Hail
and
Farewell

Cremation Ceremonies, Templates, and Tips

Gail Rubin, CT
and
Susan Fraser

Hail and Farewell:
Cremation Ceremonies, Templates, and Tips

© 2015 Light Tree Press

ISBN-13: 978-0-9845962-7-0

Light Tree Press
P.O. Box 36987
Albuquerque, NM 87176-6987

www.LightTreePress.com

Catullus 101

Carried through many nations and over many seas,
I arrive, brother, for these wretched funeral rites,
So that I might present you with the last tribute of death
And speak in vain to silent ash,
Since Fortune has carried you, yourself, away from me.
Alas, poor brother, unfairly taken away from me,
Now in the meantime, nevertheless, these things which in
the ancient custom of ancestors
Are handed over as a sad tribute to the rites
Receive, dripping much with brotherly weeping.
And forever, brother, hail and farewell.

This elegiac poem was written approximately 57 C.E. by the Roman poet Gaius Valerius
Catullus to honor his brother's cremated remains.

_T_ABLE OF CONTENTS

Foreword

BY GAIL RUBIN, CT
The Doyenne of Death®

Cremation as a form of disposition has grown dramatically in the United States over the past few decades. Why? Individuals and families have left their hometown roots. Catholics and Jews have eased their traditional resistance to cremation. As the economy struggles along and funeral prices rise, the relatively lower cost of cremation has made its popularity soar.

In 2014, 46.7 percent of those who died in the United States chose cremation. In some Western states, more than 75 percent of those who die each year are cremated. The national average for cremation rates in the United States is predicted to exceed 50 percent by 2016, according to the Cremation Association of North America. Back in 1985, less than 15 percent of the population chose cremation. Things certainly have changed!

The United States currently lags behind other countries in cremation rates. In the United Kingdom, the average is 78 percent. In countries with large populations of Hindus and Buddhists, cremation is the preferred disposition method. India has an 80 percent cremation rate, and in Japan, 99 percent of those who die are cremated.

People perceive the cremation process as simpler and easier than a traditional funeral. You'll learn that there are still many steps to arranging a cremation. Just because the disposition method changes, it doesn't negate the need for a ritual to say goodbye to our beloved dead. A "simpler" process doesn't fill the hole in our hearts and lives when someone we love dies.

Why Have a Memorial Service?

Maybe you don't care what people do about you after your death. After all, you won't be around to enjoy the party. But the people who love you care deeply.

It's not your place to go around telling people you don't want a memorial service when you die. If people didn't love you, they wouldn't go to the trouble. Memorial services may be about the person who died, but they are for the living — to remember and celebrate the life of the deceased and support each other through a time of grief.

Funerals — or memorial services if the body isn't present at the event — provide the opportunity for family and friends to come together in support, remember and share stories about the dearly departed, and celebrate his or her character and contributions. These dispatching ceremonies provide an appropriate closing chapter in the book of a person's life.

We need rituals to help recognize loss. Grief counselors see this time and again. A family doesn't hold a funeral, and six months later, family members are still having a hard time with grieving and healing. Clinicians I know through the Association for Death Education and Counseling see this with alarming frequency.

Part of this trend can be attributed to the decline of religion in American life. The number of "nones" — people with no religious affiliation — has climbed steadily in the 21st century. A study conducted by the Pew Research Center in 2012 found that one-fifth of the U.S. population, and one-third of adults under the age of 30, were religiously unaffiliated. When the study was updated in 2015, they found the Christian share of the U.S. population dramatically declining and the number of "nones" growing.

For the religiously unaffiliated, the question becomes: What do you do when there's a death in the family? If you don't relate to the rituals tied to a church, synagogue, mosque or other house of worship, how do you regain wholeness in the face of great loss?

There's a growing number of professional Certified Funeral Celebrants in the United States available to fill this religious gap. Celebrants are trained and certified to meet the needs of families — both religious and nonreligious — during their times of loss.

Celebrants provide completely personalized memorial services that reflect the personality and lifestyle of the deceased. They incorporate those unique stories, songs and experiences that defined that person, and they have a library of resources available for readings, music, ceremonies and personal touches. Celebrants know how to construct a meaningful, memorable "good goodbye" for all kinds of situations.

The bereavement process starts with the recognition and realization that someone has died. The memorial service provides an opportunity to remember and tell stories about the person, to come to terms with the reality of death, to reaffirm beliefs, and to release the spirit of the deceased. Remembering and reaffirming generate stories and laughter; realizing and releasing prompt healing tears and goodbyes.

Psychologists note a number of reasons why these rituals are important. They make the dead "safely dead," dispatched with proper ceremony to rest in peace. They confirm that the deceased and their survivors matter and that the community will continue. They provide structure in the midst of chaos and disorder, and they assure communal support for survivors during a stressful time.

You don't need to have a body to celebrate the life of the dearly departed. With burial, you need to take care of disposition within a week to 10 days. With cremation, a memorial service can be scheduled weeks or even months later, opening up a whole range of creative possibilities. However, to reap the healing benefits of a memorial service, you may want to hold the event within the first few weeks after the death, when grief is still fresh and the act of creating a service can help the process of mourning.

During my 30 Funerals in 30 Days Challenge in 2012, I attended a memorial luncheon in a bowling alley bar. The wife of the man who had died did not hold a funeral for him. Perhaps he had spent too much time at the bar in the bowling alley.

However, the bartender at the bowling alley knew his friends wanted to say goodbye to him. She organized a potluck luncheon, placed a death notice in the newspaper, and set up a memorial display in a corner of the bar for the event. The man's friends shared stories, commended the man's charitable and civic activities, and raised a toast in his honor. Attendees left feeling better, having celebrated the life of their friend.

This book is designed to help you create meaningful, memorable life celebrations and memorial services for those who choose cremation. There's a wide world of options to consider. And the best time to consider and discuss these options is today, when death seems far in the future.

Now, while you can still laugh in the face of death, learn what you need to know. Before the Grim Reaper comes to call, become an informed consumer. After all, if your car died, you wouldn't run right out and buy the first automobile at the first dealership you visited, would you? No; chances are, you would think about what you wanted in your next vehicle, figure out your budget, do a little research online, and check out the prices at a couple of dealerships.

It's the same with planning a memorial service. Just as talking about sex won't make you pregnant, talking about funerals won't make you dead. Use this book to create meaningful, memorable "good goodbyes" for those you love.

Gail Rubin, The Doyenne of Death®
Certified Thanatologist and Certified Funeral Celebrant
Albuquerque, New Mexico
October 2015

THE CREMATION PROCESS
AND
DISPOSITION ISSUES

THE CREMATION PROCESS

Cremation reduces a body to brittle bone fragments that are ground into a fine grit called cremated remains, sometimes called cremains. In fire-based cremation, the body is placed in a special furnace called a retort, which is designed to burn away or evaporate any part of the body that is flammable or liquid. Any dental work, joint replacements or medically implanted pins and screws that survive the fire are screened out of the remains. Most of this metal is recycled.

The body must be placed in a container before being put into the retort; this is usually either a cardboard box or a wooden casket built for cremation. Those who want a funeral with an open casket followed by cremation have the option of using rental caskets, which are designed with removable beds and combustible liners. There are also new combustible caskets that are lightweight yet strong; these are made of recycled wood fiber, which is available in a wide variety of finishes. These caskets offer a range of aesthetic options and burn more efficiently than wood.

The most basic container for holding cremated remains from the retort is a heavy plastic bag in a cardboard box — often an eight-inch cube. There is a wide range of decorative memorial containers available to hold cremated remains: urns of metal, stone, ceramic, wood and other materials, as well as biodegradable containers that can be used for burial or a send-off into a body of water.

ARRANGING A CREMATION

For a body to be cremated, the deceased must have preauthorized the process before his or her death, or a family member must authorize cremation. If the deceased preauthorized cremation, the funeral home may have a photo identification on file, which will serve as acceptable identification. Otherwise, a family member or named representative may be asked to visually identify the body before it is cremated to avoid any mix-up of bodies. This is done so family members can be sure the remains they receive are indeed those of their loved one.

The funeral home must obtain the exact legal name of the deceased for the death certificate — no nicknames. The body is tagged with a metal disc that identifies the deceased and survives the fire. This tag stays with the body and the remains throughout the cremation process. Pacemakers and other mechanical devices using batteries are removed before cremation, as they can explode in the retort.

In most states, the local county medical examiner's office, or sometimes the local health department, must issue a permit before cremation can occur. This step is taken to ensure that cremating the body will not prematurely destroy evidence that may be needed in a criminal case. The fee for a cremation permit varies depending on the municipality; fees may be as low as $25 and as high as $350.

Cremation is an irreversible process that destroys DNA and the individual biomarkers in cells. Funeral directors will often make this point before proceeding with the cremation, much to some families' annoyance. Some funeral homes now offer a service to save the deceased's DNA prior to cremation, should the family wish to access it someday for ancestry or medical reasons.

FREE CREMATION OPTIONS

For those who want to minimize the cost of cremation, donating your body to science helps foster medical education and research while providing cremation at no cost to the family. Many medical schools and national research organizations will foot the bill for transportation, cremation and a death certificate. They will either return the cremated remains to the family or scatter the ashes.

Cadavers are used for surgical education, disease research, creating and improving medical instrumentation and studying tissues and organs. Most medical schools and national body donation services only accept whole body donations, with the exception of corneal donations. The rest of the body must be intact for students to dissect and study. Corneas, the clear surface at the front of the eye, help save eyesight through corneal transplants. Corneas can be harvested at the funeral home.

Organ donation is a separate program and procedure that helps save lives in the event of a tragic accident. The organ donation choice is usually indicated on a driver license. However, organ donors do not automatically get a free cremation. Free cremation is offered to those who register to donate the entire body to science, not simply agree to allow the harvesting of life-saving organs at time of death.

While the donor is still alive, when all pertinent information can easily be gathered, is the best time to pre-register with a medical school or national donation service. The donor must be a living mentally-competent adult who can sign the paperwork. University medical programs may not return cremated remains for up to two years. Keep this long timeline in mind when planning any memorial service with the anticipation of having the remains present.

Most people are eligible for body donation, regardless of age or medical conditions at death. However, there are exceptions. If the person had a communicable disease such as hepatitis, HIV/AIDS and/or tuberculosis, severe obesity or edema (fluid swelling) or the body has experienced decomposition or trauma, the body will not be eligible.

Sign up with a national donation service to serve as a Plan B, in case a medical school is unable to accept the body at time of death. Some services can accept a body after death without pre-registering, but don't count on it.

National body donation services that are accredited by the American Association of Tissue Banks include the Life Legacy Foundation, MedCure.org, and Science Care. They all provide free pick up of the body, cremation and a death certificate. These services promise the return of cremated remains within three to 12 weeks.

ENVIRONMENTAL ASPECTS

If you think cremation is environmentally friendly, consider this: The average temperature reached in a cremation retort is 1,600 to 1,800 degrees Fahrenheit. Depending on the design of the retort, the size of the body and its percentage of body fat, a fire-based cremation can take anywhere from two to six hours to complete.

A typical flame-based cremation uses approximately 25 therms of natural gas to generate 2.5 million British thermal units (BTUs) to process one body. The body may not be taking up space in a cemetery, but it will generate approximately 540 pounds (245 kilograms) of carbon dioxide (CO_2) emissions in the cremation process.

To put that in perspective, a typical home-based 5-kilowatt solar energy system in New England would take more than a month of power generation to offset the CO_2 produced by one cremation. In sunnier climates, it may still take two weeks to offset one cremation. Put another way, a cremation is the CO_2 equivalent of driving a car more than 500 miles.

There is a greener option that is starting to be adopted by the funeral industry: alkaline hydrolysis, also known as flameless cremation. This developing green alternative accelerates natural decomposition and uses a small fraction of the energy required for flame-based cremation.

Alkaline hydrolysis uses a potassium hydroxide solution to gently dissolve the body in a few hours, accelerating the natural decomposition process. The result is a sterile liquid and a sandy residue from the bones. This residue can be returned to the family, just as ashes are returned following fire-based cremation.

The liquid is pH-balanced and drained into the municipal sewer system, although it can also be a great fertilizer when sprayed on land. Since alkaline hydrolysis is a much gentler process than flame cremation, funeral directors can return up to 20 percent more bone remains to the family afterward.

The process neutralizes embalming fluid, drugs, and the body's genetic material, and it produces much less CO_2 than cremation. Following the process, titanium medical implants can be recovered intact and donated for reuse in developing countries by organizations such as Doctors Without Borders, an option not available after flame cremation.

Although only a handful of funeral homes in the United States currently offer the alkaline hydrolysis process, the Mayo Clinic has successfully used it for many years to dispose of bodies donated for scientific research.

MAILING AND SHIPPING ISSUES

If you need to send the ashes of a person or a pet somewhere, the U.S. Postal Service offers the only legal method of shipping cremated remains domestically or internationally, using their Priority Mail Express® Service.

FedEx and United Parcel Service (UPS) will not knowingly ship cremated remains.

You might be distributing cremated remains among many relatives, or perhaps you are shipping remains to an artisan or craftsperson to be made into jewelry, blown glass or other kinds of artwork. Here are a few tips to know before you head to the Post Office:

1. You'll need to pack the remains in two containers – an inner container and an outer container (i.e. a box) with padding between the two.
2. The inner container must be strong and durable. It must be properly sealed and siftproof. A siftproof container prevents loose powder from leaking or sifting out during transit.
3. While not a requirement, it's recommended that the inner container be placed in a sealed plastic bag.

4. For international shipments, the inner container must be a durable funeral urn and the appropriate customs declaration forms must be filled out.
5. Use padding around the inner container, such as bubble wrap or foam peanuts, to prevent breakage during transportation.
6. The outer container is a cardboard shipping box. You might want to line it with plastic, in case there's leakage from the inner container.
7. Make sure there is no movement of the contents within the shipping box.
8. Before closing and sealing the shipping box, place a slip of paper with the address and contact information for both the sender and recipient inside the box. That way, if the label on the outside is obscured, postal employees can still find out where it's to go by looking inside the box.
9. Clearly identify the contents as cremated remains! The post office provides a handy free label to put on the outer container.
10. Ship the box via Priority Mail Express Service, which includes tracking. You wouldn't want to lose a loved one in transit.

For more detailed mailing directions, visit this page at the USPS website: http://about.usps.com/publications/pub139.pdf

AIR TRAVEL WITH CREMATED REMAINS
If you are traveling by air with cremated remains, follow Transportation Security Administration (TSA) and airline rules to avoid problems in transit.

Passengers may transport remains as part of their carry-on luggage or, depending on the airline, as checked baggage. Check with your airline prior to heading to the airport when deciding whether or not to pack those remains in a checked suitcase.

Some airlines require a death certificate or official transit letter from the funeral/cremation provider. As of October 2014, those airlines include Delta, JetBlue and United – check with your carrier to make sure you know the latest regulations. As of June 2015, Southwest only allows remains in carry-on luggage.

To go through the TSA security checkpoint, the container must be made of material that allows screeners to see clearly what is inside using an X-ray machine. A temporary container made of lightweight plastic or wood or a cardboard box with a heavy plastic bag liner is considered "security friendly." Avoid any lead-lined containers.

Documentation from a funeral home is not sufficient to allow a cremation container through a security checkpoint if the urn contents cannot be viewed by X-ray. If a TSA officer can't determine that the container does not contain a prohibited item, the remains will not be permitted through the checkpoint.

TSA says their officers are not allowed to open a container that the x-ray machine cannot see through, even if a passenger requests the container be opened. However, there have been horror stories of TSA agents opening containers and spilling remains at checkpoints and in checked baggage.

Avoid this emotional affront by using a lightweight temporary container for travel and secure a permanent urn at your final destination. The funeral home or cremation service can advise you on the type of container to select when claiming remains from the crematorium.

CREMATION DISPOSITION ISSUES

One of the key cost savings offered by cremation is that you don't have to buy a burial plot, a niche or another permanent resting place for cremated remains. There are plenty of other options.

You can keep the remains in a container at home. You can bury them in your backyard (see the Legal Issues section for guidelines). Or you can share the remains among family members in any number of creative ways.

It's estimated that close to 40 percent of cremations culminate in a scattering of the remains, either on land or water. Let's look at the social, ethical, emotional, religious and legal issues related to the scattering of cremated remains.

SOCIAL, ETHICAL AND EMOTIONAL ISSUES

One big reason people give for wanting to have their ashes scattered is societal mobility. When family members live across the country, why would they take the trouble to go visit a grave? If the deceased's remains are dispersed in a place the person loved to visit, it follows that the general vicinity of the scattering would be a meaningful destination for any family members who want to take the time and effort to visit.

Think carefully about any family discord that might arise over scattering versus giving the remains a permanent resting spot. Chester French Stewart, chairman emeritus of the FRENCH Family of Companies, which includes several funeral homes in Albuquerque, tells the story of a young woman who flew from New York to New Mexico to visit the grave of her grandfather. However, in accordance with his instructions, Grandpa had been cremated and his remains scattered in the mountains, with no record of the exact spot.

"She began weeping," recounted Stewart, "and said, 'How could you do such a thing as this?' Our company has found over the years that when the family doesn't have a permanent place of remembrance to visit, they often regret it. While they're honoring the request of the person who died, I usually tell people it's really worth thinking about taking at least a part of the cremated remains and putting them in a permanent place to visit. Because often, it skips a generation; it's not so much the kids who are interested, but the grandkids who are trying to find their roots."

Is it ethical to scatter ashes? Will other people affected by the death object to the scattering? If there's conflict over dispersing, it's important to reach a resolution to prevent ongoing discord. As Stewart's story illustrates, a person may not know if the scattering of his or her remains will cause emotional distress to the younger members of the family.

Making the right decision involves several considerations. The agreement of family members is one element. The wishes of the deceased is another. Treating the remains respectfully and dispersing them in a manner and place that honors the deceased is important. If the scattering will take place on private land, permission must be obtained from the land owner. If it is family-owned land, obtaining permission should not be an issue.

RELIGIOUS ISSUES

Cremation has a long history, stretching back to biblical times. Generally speaking, monotheists buried their dead and polytheists cremated. The ancient Greeks and Romans practiced cremation. The Christians and Jews of the same era preferred burial.

Hindus and Buddhists traditionally cremate their dead. The Ganges River in India is considered a holy site for cremation by pyre. The ashes are then scattered in the river. Unfortunately, the popularity of cremation and scattering here has contributed to making the Ganges one of the most polluted rivers in the world.

The tendency of Christians and Jews to avoid cremation is in part attributable to resurrection beliefs that originated in Judaism. The belief is that at the end of days, on Judgment Day, all of those who once lived will be restored to their bodies, renewed and better than before. With this in mind, traditional Jews go to great lengths to keep the body as intact as possible at burial, even saving and burying amputated limbs for later reunion with the rest of the body.

The question is: If you cremate the body and grind the bones into powder, how can there be a body to be resurrected into? One could argue that if God can restore your spirit to your body, even though what's left is just the bones, why couldn't God further pull those ground-up remains together to recreate a better body?

It's important that both the body and the soul or spirit be treated with dignity. The Catholic Church and the Reform branch of Judaism are open to cremation, although both religions still prefer that the cremated remains be given a permanent final resting place.

LEGAL ISSUES

There is no U.S. law against scattering cremated remains. However, there are various local rules and regulations, depending on where you live. In most states, you may disperse cremated remains as you wish.

There are no state or federal cremation police on the lookout for ash-scattering parties.

California and South Dakota have complicated rules about scattering. A helpful resource for a state-by-state breakdown of funeral rules is "Final Rights: Reclaiming the American Way of Death," by Joshua Slocum and Lisa Carlson.

The policies on scattering ashes in national parks, national forests or Bureau of Land Management acreage vary for individuals versus commercial scattering services. For individuals hiking into Forest Service land to scatter ashes, it's essentially a "don't ask, don't tell" policy. If you feel you need a piece of paper to be legal, you can get special use permits to scatter human cremated remains in many national parks. They are available through the National Park Service's website, www.nps.gov.

As long as you don't try to erect any memorials on public land, scattering cremated remains is generally OK. Just don't do it in front of a park ranger. And when you do the disposition, actually scatter the remains; don't just dump them in a pile.

Cremation and scattering goes against the religious traditions of many Native American tribes. Be aware of tribal land boundaries, and avoid scattering on their land out of respect for their traditions.

More stringent policies apply to commercial scattering services operating in the air or on the sea. Professional services are responsible for following all regulations.

If you are scattering at the beach — on the sand, not in the water — be considerate of sunbathers who will be there after you. Scatter remains in the dunes, not on the shore. That way, folks won't lay their beach blankets on Mom's ashes.

When it comes to scattering remains in the water, regulations vary. California regulations dictate removing the cremated remains from the container and scattering at least 500 feet from shore and not from any bridge or pier.

Environmental Protection Agency regulations dictate that scattering must take place at least three miles offshore, but again, there are no cremation police to enforce this regulation. There are a number of biodegradable urns designed to dissolve in water, so you can conduct a graceful send-off without getting remains blown onto your clothing or in your face.

Individuals may legally scatter cremated remains on their own private land. Burial of remains in a container, if they will remain on the property, must be disclosed to any potential buyers of the property. So, go ahead and bury Dad's cremated remains in your backyard. Just remember to remove the remains if you sell the property, or alert any future homeowners to the presence of those remains, so there are no rude surprises.

MEMORIALIZATION

Instead of scattering cremated remains, you can give ashes a permanent resting place. Cemeteries and churches offer a growing number of ways to economically honor a loved one's wishes to be cremated and give the living a place to visit the remains of the dead.

Choices include:

- Columbaria or urn niches inside a mausoleum: Some cemeteries have buildings with rooms of glass-fronted niches that enable family to visit and admire the beautiful urns of loved ones.

- Cremation gardens: Cemeteries are adding gardens with stone walls containing multiple niches, flower beds with dedicated burial areas and themed areas with sculptures.

- Ossuaries: Some churches and cemeteries offer communal final resting places for the remains of many. It can be a space behind a wall, a well, a building or other structure, with nameplates to identify the deceased.

- Scattering gardens: Some cemeteries provide a garden area for scattering cremated remains where the name of the deceased can be inscribed on a nearby wall or memorial plaque.

- Cremated remains burial plots: Cemeteries also offer small burial plots and markers for the burial of cremated remains.

2

TYPES OF CREMATION ASH SCATTERING

When planning a memorial ceremony for a loved one, the family needs to decide what to do with the cremated remains. Families have a wide range of options for putting the remains to rest.

Some people prefer to scatter ashes instead of keeping them at home or placing them in a cemetery columbarium. Many families opt to scatter the ashes in a variety of ways, depending on their cultural and religious preferences, as well as their loved ones' final wishes.

There are few rules or laws regulating the disposition of ashes on land, on water, or in the air. Your choices are largely left up to your own discretion. If your loved one wanted to have his or her ashes scattered at sea or buried in a favorite place, most families will endeavor to fulfill those wishes.

Cremation memorial services are often unbound by social conventions. Families can choose precisely how they want to carry out the proceedings, with as much or as little formality as they like.

This chapter covers six different ways to scatter or bury ashes, including casting, burial in a trench, raking, scattering over water, aerial scattering and green burial.

URNS FOR SCATTERING AND BURIAL

Anyone who browses for urns for scattering, burial or as a keepsake might be surprised by the wonderful variety available. Urns are made from a wide selection of materials, including glass, porcelain, bronze, sand, wood and many biodegradable materials.

When purchasing urns, families should consider all their plans for the ashes. If you intend to scatter or bury the ashes completely, you may only need one urn. Urns that will remain with the family following the scattering ceremony can be as unique and individual as the loved one you are honoring. Urns can feature themes such as sports, automobiles or natural symbols that memorialize a loved one's lifetime interests. Urns are available in different materials, shapes and sizes to suit your taste, and some offer an opportunity to display a photo of your loved one or your family.

For a trenching or green burial ceremony, families should choose urns that will biodegrade fully. Natural urns come in different shapes and styles, incorporating artwork or other attributes that may reflect the deceased's own personal interests or a nature theme. They range from box and pillow designs composed of 100 percent biodegradable materials to urns made of sweet grass and palm.

Many people like the idea of returning a person's ashes to the earth so that they may one day nourish life again. To meet those needs, some urns include a tree seed or seedling whereas others allow you to place your own selected seeds in the containers along with the ashes. As the seeds sprout or seedling develops, a lasting memorial is created that can provide beauty and enjoyment to others, often for decades to come.

Although complete scattering or burial is a popular option, plenty of families choose to reserve a portion of the ashes as a keepsake or to share with other relatives and friends. Small keepsake urns hold a minute amount of ashes. You might select a small urn similar to the urn used for burial; alternatively, the family may choose to have the ashes put into memorial jewelry or ornaments to give to those left behind.

The most important thing is to choose an urn or keepsake that suits the family's needs as well as the personality of the deceased.

CASTING

Casting is one of the most popular and longstanding methods of memorializing a loved one. Casting refers to the scattering of a deceased person's ashes over the water, on the ground or into the air. Ashes may be cast over the ocean, near a vacation spot that has special meaning, or into the air as a symbolic "letting go," freeing the spirit to travel to a life beyond.

The History of Casting – Casting was a popular practice among both the ancient Greeks and the ancient Romans. Excavations and early texts reveal that in the ancient Greek city of Lefkandi, friends and loved ones customarily scattered a small amount of the cremated ashes across the ground in a memorial service to the departed.

Perhaps one of the most recognizable traditional rites of casting, still in practice today, is the ancient Hindu practice of scattering cremated remains in the Ganges River. In the Hindu faith, being cast into the Ganges is very desirable, and permanent pyre supports line the river in some holy cities. Similarly, in Bali, high-ranking people and others deemed worthy enough are cremated on special towers, and their remains are then scattered across the water.

Modern Casting Ceremonies – Most contemporary casting ceremonies begin with a brief speech or eulogy, music or a poetry reading. Some prefer to recite passages or personal memories while casting the ashes over the ground, onto the water or into the air. Many take photos to serve as keepsakes afterward. Depending on where the ceremony takes place, candles and photos may be used to personalize the service. Or a wreath or individual flowers can be placed into water along with the ashes. You can mix the ashes with wildflower seeds or birdseed before casting them, to add a touch of the natural environment.

Casting can be performed from a boat or from the air via a privately chartered plane or helicopter. Before scattering ashes openly in a public place, contact local officials to find out about any relevant regulations. This will help ensure that your memorial is as beautiful as you intend.

TRENCHING

Unlike the act of scattering the ashes gently on the ground, in the water or in the air, some families prefer to trench their loved ones' remains. In a trenching ceremony, a shallow trench or pit is dug in the ground, often in a place of remembrance. Once the trench is dug, the cremated remains are placed in the trench and then covered over with soil. Trenching may be performed by a funeral service provider or the family, depending on the regulations for disposing of ashes in your area and your own individual preferences.

History of Trenching – As with casting, trenching's popularity also extends deep into the past. From 1,000 B.C. to 750 B.C., the Greeks used trenching almost exclusively in their final ceremonies. The ashes of the deceased were placed in special urns called amphorae. In the earliest ceremonies, the urn was placed in the center of the trench. Pyre debris was swept into the hole beside it before being covered with earth. In later ceremonies, a separate, deeper hole for the amphora was dug at one end of the trench. These later designs were known as trench-and-hole cremations.

During the Roman Empire, cremation was mainstream, with many families choosing to bury cremated remains in a trench or pit afterward. Excavations at Roman settlements in Britain indicate that ashes were often placed in wooden buckets, sometimes accompanied by objects and personal belongings, before being buried in trenches.

Modern Trenching Ceremonies – Today's trenching ceremonies are highly personal memorials, as varied as the land in which the remains are placed. Families often choose to add their own touches to the trenching service, forming shallow trenches in the shape of the deceased's initials, a heart or a short message before scattering the ashes inside and covering them with soil. Sometimes, families display a keepsake or biodegradable urn during the service before the ashes are put in the trench.

Trenching is popular along beaches, where the rising tide is allowed to gently wash the remains to sea. Ceremonies may be timed to coincide with the tide to allow loved ones to watch as the remains return to the sea. Many people decide to take photos of the ceremony or to encircle the area with candles, both of which can be distributed as keepsakes. Those in attendance may join hands around the trench and recite a poem or recall memories of their loved one.

RAKING

While many people choose to scatter cremated remains or bury them in the earth, others prefer to incorporate the ashes lightly into the soil. This way, the ashes may contribute to the environment by providing nutrients for flowers and other plants. This process is known as raking.

History of Raking – Archeological excavations reveal that although ancient civilizations buried complete urns, they also sometimes incorporated the ashes back into the soil. Far back in history, cremation rites and rituals varied markedly from one province or settlement to another. Raking provided a way to return a loved one's remains to the earth for all eternity. Raking may have been especially important to more nomadic groups, where deeper pit burials were unwarranted and carrying ashes would have proved too cumbersome.

Modern Raking Ceremonies – Today, raking ceremonies rely heavily on symbolism to promote understanding. Many ceremonies take place in scattering grounds known as "memory gardens," places set aside by communities, religious institutions and public cemeteries for the specific purpose of scattering, trenching or raking ashes. As an alternative, beach locations are popular, as they allow the remains to be washed to sea. Check the local regulations before holding a raking ceremony at any location to ensure you do not run afoul of any laws.

Raking may be performed by a spouse or child of the deceased or by friends and loved ones. This offers an opportunity to pay respects and achieve a sense of closure for everyone involved. Depending on where the ceremony takes place, some family members may wish to scatter seeds along with the ashes to provide a living memory.

Some families like to maintain a degree of the traditional during the ceremony, with music, eulogies or poetry readings. Others take pictures and notes from guests to create a memory book for the grieving family. Many memory gardens offer opportunities to erect stones or other memorials, including benches or bird feeders. Following the ceremony, you may choose to keep the rake or donate it to a community gardening program.

SCATTERING OVER WATER

Water is a symbol of infinity, traveling in a continual loop from the earth's surface up to the heavens through evaporation and then falling once again to earth as rain or snow. The idea of sending one's ashes into the water is appealing, given the importance of water in many historic and modern cultures and religions. This method of scattering involves depositing the ashes directly on the surface of a large body of water or distributing them into the water through the use of a dissolvable urn.

History of Scattering Over Water – From a cultural standpoint, scattering a loved one's ashes over the water is often considered a symbolic representation of the ethereal spirit being carried away from the constraints of the physical body. It has a long history, especially in Asian cultures. Hinduism teaches that the goddess Ganga descended from heaven to save the spirits of the dead from the netherworld. Her path from heaven to earth also provides a path for the deceased to enter heaven. Committing the ashes of the deceased to the Ganges River in India enables people to begin their journey to the next life. Likewise, in Tibet, scattering ashes over a lake or stream has long been a common practice for Buddhists.

Modern Water-Scattering Ceremonies – Scattering ashes over the water is usually done from a boat, from the air, or at the water's edge. When done from a boat, plane or helicopter, the operator of the boat or aircraft or another officer generally performs the scattering to ensure that it is done safely. Of course, some families may elect to pilot their own boats or planes if someone in the family is licensed to do so. As for any type of public ash dispersal, you may want to contact local authorities before casting the ashes over water to make sure your plans are compliant with the area's laws and regulations.

Many ceremonies include poems, music or spontaneous recitations or comments by those in attendance. Lighting candles or casting flowers, petals or wreaths on the water along with the ashes are lovely choices, as well. Taking photos or video of the ceremony to send to each person involved is a thoughtful way to honor your loved one long after the scattering ceremony ends.

AERIAL SCATTERING

Like scattering over water, aerial scattering involves the dispersal of a loved one's ashes over a large area. This method has grown in popularity in recent years as more people look for ways to cast ashes over a wider geographic area or location. Aerial scattering of ashes can be done by plane, helicopter, hang glider or even hot air balloon. Some people use skydivers to disperse ashes over a specific area.

History of Aerial Scattering – Scattering ashes by air is a relatively modern concept, since it relies on air travel technology. While once the purview of private or military pilots and their families, today aerial scattering is the choice of many men and women who wish to have their ashes truly become dust in the wind.

Many former military members choose aerial scattering from the same type of aircraft they once piloted or flew in. In 2014, one World War II veteran had his ashes scattered from a B-25 bomber, the same type of aircraft he piloted for 50 missions in the South Pacific during World War II.

Modern Aerial Scattering Ceremonies – Aerial ash scattering is much more widely available now than it was even a few decades ago. Some ash-scattering service providers offer flights over historic landmarks, parks or other areas. A family that enjoyed happy memories vacationing in a national park, at the seashore, or in another location may find comfort in having a loved one's ashes scattered by air over the area.

Ceremonies for aerial scattering often begin with a small service on the ground, most commonly at the airport prior to takeoff. In some cases, one or more family members may decide to accompany the ashes during the flight; other families may leave the flight to the pilot and any additional crew. Some pilots release ashes directly from the cockpit while others use funnel or tube devices to release them from the outside of the plane. Low-altitude flights and dispersal from hot air balloons, from gliders or by skydivers usually do not spread the ashes over as wide an area.

While some ceremonies are held in view of the ash-release location, a few aerial services involve releasing the ashes in remote areas that cannot be viewed from the ground. Some aerial scattering companies will take photographs of the ashes as they are released or issue a certificate noting the date and time of release to provide a lasting memento of the ceremony for loved ones to cherish.

GREEN BURIAL

As people's thoughts turn to concern for the environment, more families seek earth-friendly alternatives for the final disposition of cremated remains. Green burials use biodegradable materials that naturally dissolve into the soil over time. In recent years, people have chosen green burials as a way to reconnect with the earth and decrease their impact on the environment. When you select a cremation without embalming, combined with a biodegradable urn, you help honor your loved one's commitment to improving the natural world.

History of Green Burials – The origin of green burials is as old as mankind. Long before there were embalming fluids, bodies were laid to rest in the soil, where they gradually decomposed over time in a manner that nurtured the soil and all living things. During the Renaissance, scientific researchers began studying forms of embalming as a way to preserve organs for scientific study.

It was not until the 19th century that embalming became common-place. Embalming initially was used during the Civil War as a way to preserve bodies for transport back to deceased soldiers' homes for final interment. Over time, many communities began requiring embalming, believing it to prevent the spread of certain diseases that might be transmitted after death. Green burials do not employ embalming chemicals, thus allowing for a more natural decomposition.

Modern Green Burial Ceremonies – Modern green burial ceremonies often incorporate many of the same rituals and practices as traditional burial services, including eulogies and hymns. They may begin with a gathering to remember the deceased, similar to a viewing ceremony. The funeral service itself can be designed to suit your loved one's wishes, as well as those of the family. At the end of the ceremony, you may want to invite all those in attendance to the grave site for a grave-side ceremony. Or you may reserve that option for family members and other close friends. Some families choose to hold a simple service at the graveside without a funeral service.

Depending on the location of the burial, you might consider providing flower seeds for attendees to spread on top of the site once the urn is interred, much as flowers are placed on top of a casket in a more traditional ceremony. Many families use candles or release doves or butterflies during the ceremony. In lieu of flowers, ceremony hosts often ask friends and family to donate to nature-related charities or to provide bags of pet food to local animal shelters. Some green burial sites offer opportunities for donations to fund tree plantings, birdhouses or benches. If the ultimate goal is to promote a better world, contributing to new growth is a wonderful way to close the ceremony.

CONCLUSION

As with funerals, scattering and burial ceremonies are important rites of passage for the family of someone who has died. Whether families choose casting, trenching, raking, scattering over water, aerial scattering or a green burial, the ultimate goal is to give everyone a chance to say goodbye as the ashes are put in their final resting place.

The sending of ashes back to the natural world through one of these methods is symbolic of the cyclical nature of life. In the end, the ceremony and scattering provides loved ones with the closure they need to move forward through the grieving process, with beautiful memories of the one they leave behind.

3

LIFE CELEBRATION STORIES

The following stories vividly demonstrate the wide range of meaningful memorial celebrations that families and friends may organize to say goodbye to their loved ones. In each case, those making the plans drew upon the unique characteristics of the departed to create a fitting life celebration. Following the stories are some practical considerations to keep in mind when arranging different types of ceremonies.

A MEMORIAL IN THE MOUNTAINS

At 25 years old, K. was an outstanding athlete, rich in life, with an undeniable love for people. He majored in biology at Lewis and Clark College in Portland, Oregon. There, he became a member of the Portland Mountain Rescue team, saving many people and helping even more. He later moved to California and became a member of the Mammoth Mountain Ski Patrol, where he was a first responder who helped thousands in harsh conditions. He spent summers working with the American Alpine Institute, eventually becoming a well-respected guide.

Above all, K. was a natural mentor. He always encouraged others to succeed in their own life ambitions. He climbed 20,000+ foot mountains in the Andes of South America and developed a climbing guide and instruction manual to reach the top of 14,494-foot Mount Whitney.

Young K. taught others about many aspects of the wilderness, and he taught those who mountaineered with him about themselves.

K. was avid about snow, and he studied avalanches, which is not common among mountaineers. For him it was a passion — a science he took to new heights of understanding. In his continuous pursuit to learn more, he took advanced avalanche training to study the hydraulics of when, how and why avalanches occur.

K. died pursuing what he loved to do. He lost his life in a helicopter crash, along with three other passengers and their pilot, while en route to an eight-day avalanche training course in the Kootenays of British Columbia, Canada.

K.'s ashes were scattered on the summit of Mount Hood in Oregon, where he had saved and helped so many souls. On many occasions, he liked to summit this beautiful stratovolcanic peak to eat, view the other Cascade peaks around him, and fly kites. From atop Mount Hood, he would ski down through the Pearly Gates, fly over the Bergschrund crevasse and make his way back to the Timberline Lodge, where he worked.

The night before the scattering ceremony, many of K.'s friends and family joined together at the Timberline Lodge at the base of Mount Hood. Many people from different communities joined together to talk and reminisce about the memories they held of K. There were people from his college, Portland Mountain Rescue team members, Mammoth Ski Patrol members, California friends, American Alpine Institute staff members, and his parents, among many others.

Early the next morning, way before the sun was up — as is typical in mountaineering — the participants found different ways up the mountain. With the abundance of snow, even in May, some took to snow shoes; others simply walked or took the Sno-Cat that was transporting people to the top of the ski lift, from where they could ascend further. The group was all over the place, spread out between the lodge and the Hogsback, a short ridge everyone could reach. Everyone seemed to converge at the right place and the right time.

Since many of those attending the scattering were not climbers and lacked experience, it was decided to do a partial scattering ceremony right there on the Hogsback. At this time, K.'s father had a private moment with his son — several minutes of quiet time. He made the first cast of the remains, his wife cast next, and a few words were said. The remainder of K.'s ashes, in his cremation urn, were passed off to those who could successfully make the trip up to the summit to release them.

Once the group had made it to the summit, everyone paused. The sun had risen steadily, there were very few clouds in the sky, and a slight breeze blew. They could see many of the other Cascade peaks — to the north, in Washington, they had a clear view of Mount Rainier, Mount St. Helens and Mount Adams; to the south were Oregon's Mount Jefferson and many other peaks.

It did not take long before a few kites started to fly in K.'s memory and the stories began to flow. After a short time, K.'s cremation urn was brought around for a final time. Then everyone, joyfully, many with tears in their eyes, took turns scattering K.'s ashes off the summit of Mount Hood.

The memory of this young man will live in the hearts of all those who knew him. It was once said by Sir Edmund Hillary, "It's not the mountain we conquer — but ourselves." It is amazing that at only 25 years young, K. taught so many how to conquer their inner challenges with help of the mountains. That is his legacy. That is a memorial.

BACHELOR WATER BURIAL ON A BOAT

Throughout B.'s life, he loved fishing in lakes, oceans and rivers. By the age of 5, he was making his own fishing tackle out of sticks and string. He dug up worms and made his own flies for fly-fishing. He continually begged his Dad to go fishing and, since it was in the family blood, they did so often.

His dad would take him out on weekends and as often as he could during the summer. Family summer vacations always featured great fishing spots. When B. grew up, he convinced his friends to go on fishing trips all over — to Mexico, Hawaii and a multitude of high mountain lakes. He was a true fisherman.

When B. died unexpectedly at age 23, his family discussed and then decided on cremation. B.'s family and band of friends concluded that the only fitting burial for him would be a water burial out on the deep seas, where he would love to be forever.

After a thorough online search, they found the perfect urn for B. — a biodegradable Peaceful Pillow Fishermen water burial urn. They put the majority of his ashes in this urn and the remainder into two smaller Peaceful Pillow urns for disposition in two more locations.

In the early summer, family and friends headed out of Davey's Locker in Newport Beach, California, to place the large urn in the ocean. B.'s best friend gave a touching eulogy, and, with eyes watering, B.'s father recited this poem:

We Thought of You Today

We thought of you with love today,
But that is nothing new.
We thought about you yesterday,
And days before that too.
We think of you in silence.
We often speak your name.
All we have now are memories,
And your picture in a frame.
Your memory is our keepsake,
With which we will never part.
God has you in His keeping,
We have you in our hearts.
If love alone could have saved you,
You never would have died.
In life we loved you dearly,
In death we love you still.
In our hearts you hold a place,
No one else can ever fill.
It broke our hearts to lose you,

> But you didn't go alone,
> For a part of us went with you,
> The day God took you home.
>
> —*Author unknown*

Everyone raised a glass to B. and tossed white rose petals upon the ocean. Those gathered watched the urn drift away before it slowly slipped under the surface of the water. They took their time heading back to shore as the sun set over Catalina. They reminisced with joyous stories of B. while nearby die-hard fishermen trolled for a big catch.

The remainder of B.'s ashes, in the two smaller Peaceful Pillow urns, were keepsakes for his friends and family. One went with his friends to Hume Lake, California, where he often went with his bachelor buddies. They had planned to take a trip there in the summer, and his friends carried this part of his mortal remains to stay at the lake he loved to fish.

His family took the second Peaceful Pillow to the Bighorn River in Montana, one of North America's prime fly-fishing areas for large trout. B.'s father took him there often. The family watched as the pillow floated downstream and then slowly sank under the current. A moment of silence followed, after which they enjoyed a small picnic with some of B.'s favorite snacks.

B.'s family knew he would have loved the way they celebrated his life. He will be forever missed, and not a day will go by that they won't think of him. His family and friends will warmly remember him as always being in his favorite fishing spots, trying to catch a big one.

"J. STRONG": A RIVERSIDE MEMORIAL

J. was a loving and free-spirited woman who never took life for granted. She enjoyed each day as if it were her last, spending time with her family and doing what she loved — enjoying the outdoors. Most days, she could be found reading by the river that ran behind her family's home in Kentucky. She loved the calming sound of the current as it ran downstream.

J. was a single mother of two daughters from a previous marriage. She worked in the public affairs department of a large corporation, where she met the love of her life, L. He also had a child from a previous marriage, and they bonded quickly over their children. Soon, the two were happily married and living together with their three kids.

One night, J. woke up in searing pain from horrific cramps. After a 911 call, an ambulance took her to the hospital. The results of blood work and X-rays changed her and her family's lives forever.

J. was diagnosed with primary peritoneal carcinoma, a severe type of cancer that is related to ovarian cancer. Doctors didn't know exactly how much time J. had left on Earth, but it wasn't expected to be very long.

Although she was given a time limit on her life, not once did she feel limited. For the next two and a half years, L. held J.'s hand and stood by her side through her physical and emotional trials. J. remained positive. She acknowledged the imminence of her eventual passing and began planning her own memorial ceremony. She wanted to ease the hardship on her family, and it was something she wanted to do.

Throughout J.'s battle with cancer, she met and influenced many people. One man in particular, B., was so touched by her free spirit and positive outlook on life that he took it upon himself to write a song about J. He put his lyrics to music, and she finally got to hear the song. J. was absolutely thrilled and insisted it be a part of her final arrangements. She wanted others who were battling cancer to hear the song and be inspired.

J. decided she would be cremated, and she picked out her own cremation urn. It was a beautiful white rose urn that was biodegradable and made to be set into the water. A ceremony for her passing was held at the church where J. was a longtime member. A eulogy and prayers were said while loved ones from near and far gathered to pay their respects. At the end of the ceremony, they played B.'s song, "J. Strong," bringing both a sense of joy and loss to everyone in the room.

After the church service, a small, private gathering for family and close friends was held at J. and L.'s home down by the river where she spent so many evenings. The song "J. Strong" played again in the background while L. gently placed the urn with his wife's ashes into the river. Her loved ones stood on a wooden bridge over the water, tossing rose petals into the stream.

After a few moments, the slow, calming current swept the urn beneath the water's surface. The group held a moment of silence as J.'s song continued to play, "… all I want to do from this day on is to be as strong as J."

A NATIONAL PARK SCATTERING

H., also known as Slim, was rough and tough — a natural cowboy from the day he was born. He grew up in Three Rivers, California, in the early 1900s. He spent many days and nights in the Sierra Mountains, traveling the endless trails by day and laying under the stars at night. Through the years, he made a reputation for himself as a dedicated cowboy, a great mule packer, and an experienced mountain man.

One of his favorite places was Ranger Meadow in Deadman Canyon, a glacier-carved valley in Kings Canyon National Park. The area is named after an Iberian sheep-herder who was buried in the area back in the late 1800s.

During World War II, H. joined the army. After the war, he returned to his hometown and packed mules for a well-known rancher, E. Over the years, H. and E. became great friends. They went on many hikes and trail runs, often taking E.'s young son, E. Jr., along with them. When E. Sr. passed away suddenly on the trail one day, H. traveled to pick him up on horseback and brought him home for a proper burial. Every year after E. Sr. died, Slim stopped by to see E. Jr. around the anniversary of his father's death.

After H. retired, still a bachelor, he moved to Merced, California, where he lived in the old Tioga Hotel. Although he was technically retired, he worked just as hard as he had before, as most cowboys do. He was 82 years old when he died from natural causes in his hotel room on July 25, 1989.

By this time, most of H.'s family had already passed, so his ashes were delivered to E. Jr. His remains came with the request that E. place them in a spot where he thought H. would enjoy eternal peace, rest and happiness.

E. knew right away that he needed to pack up his horse for a trip to Deadman Canyon, a place the two had agreed was one-of-a-kind. E. and his buddies set out on the trail to fulfill their scattering mission. However, the trip was in vain when realized they had forgotten the most important item — H.'s ashes!

For a good time, H.'s ashes sat in E.'s house collecting dust. E. started to worry because time wasn't going any slower, and he wasn't getting any younger. One day, while talking with a woman he knew, she mentioned that she and a friend were going to take a hike up into Deadman Canyon very soon.

E. was relieved to have the answer to his dilemma. He insisted she take Slim's ashes, along with a short eulogy for H., up the mountain with them on their trip, so he could be finally laid to rest. She agreed.

Once the women arrived at Deadman Canyon, they scattered H.'s ashes in the mountain meadow. Then they read this eulogy that E. had written for his dear friend:

In Memory of H. (Slim)

Born in 1907, died July 25, 1989, age 82 years
Early Cowboy, Mule Packer, Mountain Man and My Dear Friend

Dear Slim,

I knew of your fondness for these magnificent mountains of the Sierras that you knew and loved so well, and where you traveled its many trails so extensively.

We both talked at different times, over the years, of some of our favorite places of beauty, [and] both you and I agreed that Deadman Canyon in Ranger Meadow was about the most beautiful place we ever had the pleasure to have gazed upon.

H., when you bid us all farewell back in 1989, you had your ashes delivered to me (E. Jr.), with the charge that I would have them placed in a spot where I thought you would be happy, enjoying eternal peace and rest.

Here, this day, with the help of these two dedicated dear friends of mine, I. and K. (who delivered your ashes here and witnessed this service), your ashes are hereby placed here at this spot, forever.

I pray your eternal soul can enjoy the warm sunshine, as it rises and sets each day, and where you may watch the splendor of God's four seasons, forever to be changing as this old world turns endlessly on.

May this eagle's view of Ranger Meadow, surrounded by these majestic peaks, always be a bond of our endless friendship.

Adios Pal, 'Til We Meet Again.

—*E. Jr.*

At the end, the women sang "Amazing Grace" to finish the small scattering ceremony for dear old Slim.

MEMORIAL SAIL IN NARRAGANSETT BAY

When M. passed away in 2002, her five children and husband, T., were at her bedside. Because they were all there, she let go and left behind the painful cancer that had ravaged her body. The family honored her desire to be cremated, although they could not figure out exactly what to do with M.'s cremated remains. For a long time, they were respectfully enshrined — on the top shelf of her daughter's closet.

Ten years later, T. passed away. According to his wishes, his body was cremated, too. The family all agreed that the cremated remains of their parents should be put to rest someplace other than a closet shelf.

Together, the children considered many alternatives for scattering

31

their parents' ashes. The notion of a burial at sea resonated most powerfully. Neither M. nor T. were sailors, nor did they have a particular love of the sea, but the serenity and elegance of casting their ashes upon the water appealed to the whole family.

In the search for urns, one daughter discovered an Internet site with urns suitable for cremation burials at sea. The siblings were impressed by the unique design and beauty of the Peaceful Petal Flower water burial urn. They quickly agreed that this was the proper vehicle to convey their parents' remains to the peace of the sea.

M. and T.'s nephew offered the use of his 42-foot sloop. On a warm, late-September morning, a small group of family members set sail onto Narragansett Bay off the coast of Rhode Island. They carried the cremated remains of their mom and dad in a pair of white Peaceful Petal Flower urns. They sailed to a point in the bay that seemed right. As they dropped the sails, the air went still. The waters of the bay were soft and calm.

One of the sons, holding an urn in each palm, crouched on the swim platform at the stern. He set both urns gently upon the water. As they slowly floated in unison away from the boat, each family member cast white long-stem roses and colored rose petals on the water and said their personal farewells.

They watched in silence as the beautiful, large, white flower urns drifted off, escorted by the white roses and colorful petals. Then, very slowly, the urns began to sink beneath the surface of the water, slowly fading into the depths of the bay, leaving only the scattering of roses and petals. M. and T. were gone.

A burial at sea provides a unique and special sense of closure, in that the water receives your loved one's remains and takes them away beyond your senses. After the ceremony, the living do not walk away from a grave or a mausoleum, and there is no specific place to visit. Rather, the departed become part of the vast, peaceful sea.

29 PORTS O' CALL

This is the story of a family that choose to scatter ashes in many different places as a traveling memorial to a very special woman.

C. loved to travel the world. She started traveling when she was a young girl, crossing the United States with her parents, as well as visiting Europe. As she grew older, she traveled on her own, with friends and with family. In the years just before her passing, she traveled to Greece and Israel. Although she had planned to visit many more places, her plans changed when she suddenly became seriously ill.

After C. died, her husband, R., followed her last wishes and had her body cremated. He kept some of her cremated remains at home in a small floral urn that C. had picked out. He also secured 40 Release Wood scattering tubes for the memorial service to come.

In tribute to his wife's wanderlust, R. planned to travel the world and spread her ashes at his wife's favorite places. He laid out a plan to set off on his own and meet with family and friends along the way to scatter C.'s ashes at the locations she had longed to visit. R. hoped her spirit would be with him in this difficult time, as this was a trip they would have taken together if not for her swift passing.

The first location was close to their home, an island off the Texas Gulf Coast. At that special location, family and friends gathered for C.'s memorial service to celebrate her life. There, close family and friends scattered C.'s ashes from 11 of the Release Wood scattering tubes and remembered a remarkable wife, mother, sister and dear friend.

Everyone took their time as they scattered the ashes into the ocean from the wooden tubes and then filled the tubes back up with sand from the beach. Each person who took home a scattering tube had a lifelong remembrance of C., with her name, date of birth, and date of passing engraved into the wood.

For the next few weeks, there was lots of talk about R.'s plans to travel the world and scatter the rest of C.'s cremated remains. At each stop, R. would release C.'s ashes from a wooden tube labeled with the name of that special location. Afterward, R. would fill the tube with the sand from that place.

The family called the trip "29 Ports O' Call," visiting 29 locations with 29 scattering tubes of C.'s ashes. After much reminiscing, laughter and tears, the plans were set, and the tickets were bought.

The family raised a toast to C. in Italy, took a short hike in northern France, and drove through England to the cool beaches for a late afternoon scattering. During this special time, the family could still feel her close to them. It was a wonderful way to spend time grieving and remembering the love of C.

GRAVESIDE CEREMONY: ASHES OVER HIS HEART

L. was married almost 45 years before she lost her beloved husband, T. Many decades earlier, after their son had died of leukemia, they had bought two plots in a local cemetery. They both had all of their funeral arrangements preplanned and in order. They knew exactly what they wanted when the time came. They were to be buried side-by-side in two separate burial plots.

When T. died first, his funeral went exactly as planned. The service ended with a lone bagpiper playing the ancient Scottish folk tune, "Flowers of the Forest." The piper slowly walked into the distance, as if to show T. the way home.

L.'s life went on, and she enjoyed many years after the death of her husband. As time went by, she was blessed with grandchildren and great-grandchildren. When one grandson was born with a striking resemblance to his grandfather T. at a young age, it thrilled L. and her family.

She enjoyed a wonderful 14 years with this grandson before he suddenly died due to an undiagnosed heart disease — sadly, on Mother's Day. L. offered up her cemetery plot, so her young grandson could be close to the grandfather he so closely resembled.

She then changed her own arrangements to cremation. Her remains would be put in a cremation burial urn and placed in a special vault above her husband's casket, positioned near his heart.

L. was a lucky woman to have had many other grandchildren and great-grandchildren who brought her joy. They eased the pain of losing her son, her husband and her grandson. When L. became ill and it was her turn to pass on, most of her children and grandchildren were there by her side.

In accordance with her wishes, she was cremated, but she hadn't chosen a cremation urn. One of her grandsons, the younger brother of the grandson who had passed away years earlier, offered a special wooden chest in which he had kept small treasures over the years. This beautiful, dark wooden chest was used for her ashes.

The ceremony was simple, as L. had wanted. Family and friends gathered at her house for a vigil and reminisced about her rich 77 years of life. They talked about L.'s loving kindness and of times gone by. They held a small ceremony at the cemetery, which consoled many. The memorial cards featured L.'s portrait, her life story, and a beautiful poem. In silence, the family placed the chest filled with L.'s cremated remains into an urn burial vault, positioned in the cemetery plot right over her husband's heart. L. and T. are now together forever, with their grandson by their side.

A BEACH MEMORIAL SERVICE

A. loved living by the ocean. She delighted daily in seeing the sun glinting on the water, feeling the sand between her toes, and watching the sea rise and fall with the tides. When she was in tune with nature at the shore, she was at peace.

A. married her high school sweetheart, M., right out of high school. They supported each other through college. He became a successful attorney; she became a physical therapist. Together, they had a daughter. She loved family events at the beach, playing music around a bonfire with friends, and playing volleyball.

Tragically, at the age of 27, A. died in an automobile accident, the result of a careless driver texting and not paying attention to the traffic. A. was cremated, and her family held a memorial service on the beach in her honor.

Family and friends gathered at sunset on a Florida Gulf Coast beach. As instructed, most came dressed in beach attire or Hawaiian shirts.

Wood had already been prepared for a bonfire. The reception after the service was to be a Hawaiian luau.

The funeral director served as the master of ceremonies and introduced the celebrant, who welcomed everyone and asked them to turn off their cell phones, so they could be fully present. A.'s husband and 6-year-old daughter started the service by lighting a memorial candle in A.'s honor. The celebrant spoke about A.'s life and passions and how her life was snatched away in a careless moment on a busy afternoon by a texting driver:

> Marcel Proust said, "We say that the hour of death cannot be forecast, but when we say this we imagine that hour as placed in an obscure and distant future. It never occurs to us that it has any connection with the day already begun or that death could arrive this same afternoon, this afternoon which is so certain and which has every hour filled in advance."

After the eulogy, attendees were invited to take a small candle, light it with A.'s memorial candle, and gather around the yet-to-be-lit bonfire. As The Beach Boys' "Surfer Girl" played, everyone took a candle and a piece of saltwater taffy, A.'s favorite treat. Once everyone lit their candles, the attendees used them to light the bonfire in unison.

Around the bonfire, family and friends shared stories of a beautiful young woman and shed their tears over her loss. During the luau, everyone watched a video montage featuring pictures of A. set to the song "If I Die Young," performed by The Band Perry.

The next day, members of A.'s immediate family took a boat out into the Gulf of Mexico to put her ashes to rest. The celebrant provided final words of commitment before setting the biodegradable urn containing A.'s remains upon the water.

IZ's recording of "Over the Rainbow" played while the family tossed flowers and leis at the shell-shaped container. The urn floated for a few minutes and then slowly sank below the gentle waves.

A RESTAURANT CELEBRATION OF LIFE

J. loved Albuquerque's El Pinto Restaurant. She loved its delicious New Mexican food, the patios shaded by trees, umbrellas and flowering vines, and its many cozy indoor rooms.

J. was a writer and an adventurous woman. She played the piano and loved a glass of cognac in the evening. She had lived in Montana, Utah, Colorado, the Washington, D.C., area, Argentina and New Mexico, and she had traveled extensively.

After J. died in January, she was cremated. She wanted her ashes to be buried in Montana, next to her remarkable grandmother, who had raised her after J.'s mother died in childbirth during the delivery of J.'s younger brother. J.'s burial was to take place in the summer, and the family didn't want to wait six months to hold a memorial service.

J.'s children, who were spread out all across the country, organized a memorial service luncheon at El Pinto Restaurant for close family and J.'s Albuquerque friends a few weeks later on February 22.

Piano music on a portable stereo serenaded guests as they arrived at the reserved room in the restaurant. A poster of J.'s smiling face next to the door told them they were in the right place. Salsa and chips were available to appease the hunger of famished guests.

The celebrant made opening comments about the details of the event, introduced the family members, and showed a video created by the family with photos, videos, music and the story of J.'s life. The video tribute helped set the tone for lunch conversation. Guests were asked to talk about J. during the meal and think about a story to share.

Guests ordered whatever they wanted from the menu. They were invited to peruse a table that held photos and mementos of J.'s life, as well as her cremated remains and those of her beloved dog. During lunch, piano music played and the video tribute images cycled on a screen. The long tables were arranged in a large U shape, with guests seated on both sides.

After lunch, the celebrant delivered an in-depth eulogy, summarizing J.'s life story and characteristics. Then, the microphone was passed along to attendees. Every guest, whether family or friend, young or old, shared a story about J. The stories prompted both laughter and tears.

At the end, the celebrant provided final thoughts on J.'s life and death and J.'s grandmother's thoughts about the afterlife. In honor of her love of cognac, everyone raised a toast in her honor:

> To the life and adventures of J.: We bless your memory with great love for you, for you have written your love upon our hearts. To J.!

The family created memorial gifts for all the guests. Each person received a wineglass filled with chocolate kisses and a bookmark that featured a wildflower and a forget-me-not seed paper butterfly. The bookmark read:

> Plant this butterfly
> in loving memory of J.
> Don't weep for me because
> I'm no longer here,
> I've a date with a
> butterfly to dance in the air.
> I'll be singing in the
> sunshine, wild and free,
> playing tag with the wind
> while I'm watching over thee.

As people mingled at the end of the luncheon, many said it was an uplifting way to remember J.'s life. One of the guests said, "That was the best memorial service I've been to. I didn't feel sad or bad at the end."

There are a number of great reasons to hold a memorial service in a restaurant. If the venue was a favorite of the deceased, the setting helps set the tone to truly celebrate the person's life. The restaurant provides the needed dining space, food and drink, and some places will also have audiovisual equipment. The staff helps with the setup before the event and takes care of the cleanup afterward. The family provides the money to cover the costs, including tax and gratuity, and brings memorial items.

PRACTICAL CONSIDERATIONS FOR OUTDOOR CEREMONIES

When a person enjoyed spending time in the great outdoors, celebrating that life with a memorial service in a special place that he or she loved can be truly remarkable. By observing local laws, respecting the environment, honoring the scenery and wildlife, and creating a program that highlights all that is wonderful about the person who passed, families and friends can come together united by unconditional love.

The first thing to consider when planning an outdoor memorial service is who owns the land where the service will take place. It is important to select a location that is not encroaching on private property without the owner's knowledge or permission. If the family owns the property, make sure all members have agreed to the disposition., Permits can be obtained for scattering on many public lands, including national parks (see chapter 1).

It's generally not permitted to scatter ashes or bury them in small bodies of water such as ponds, rivers or creeks, because they may supply local community drinking water. However, the governing bodies for larger lakes may allow burial in the water, so long as the ashes are in an airtight or biodegradable container and are placed in the water a certain distance from the shore.

Hosts should plan to make the ceremony simple, without extensive technological equipment. In national or state parks, access to electricity may be limited. Also, anything brought to the water's edge must be packed up and removed upon departure. Families should visit the site before the scheduled service date to scope out seating, lighting and any possible hazards.

The ideal spot to hold a memorial ceremony near water depends on a number of factors. Consider several possible locations in the area that may offer hospitable ground, depending on the season. Many families elect to hold outdoor ceremonies in the late spring, summer or early fall to ensure the most agreeable temperature and weather patterns.

Take time to think about the loved one who has passed and the enjoyable hours that person spent in the outdoors. Did he or she love to fish on the lake? Was hiking beside a river the person's favorite pastime? The ceremony site should be large enough for everyone who wishes to attend and accessible to all.

Choosing a theme provides interesting ideas for the ceremony details. Families may opt for a theme that takes advantage of the natural environment, with local flowers, rocks and colors matching the loved one's favorite season. Or the theme could celebrate water as a purifying and regenerating gift, using programs featuring a soothing background image of a waterfall or rushing river.

What families choose to do at the service depends on their interests as well as the limitations of the selected location. To remember a fly-fisher, you may want to retrieve river rocks prior to the service. During the ceremony, you can then encourage friends and family members to put the rocks back into the water as they recount a favorite memory of the one who is gone.

With the permission of the administrators or owners of the property, attendees can leave a lasting memory of their final goodbye. Some families construct a cairn — a pile of natural rocks — near the place where their loved one's ashes are put to rest or scattered.

Or they may plant a tree or other foliage in an approved location as a symbol that the person they miss will live on forever in their hearts. Some people like to place a local water flower, such as a water lily, to take root and grow at the edge of a lake or pond.

For easy setup and takedown, avoid large or complex decorations. Plan for possible inclement weather, and bring canopies or tents just in case. Set up a small table with a guest book and pictures of the recently deceased. One idea is to collect rocks and bring markers for loved ones to use in writing messages of love and hope for the grieving family. The rocks may be used as mementos back home or can line a garden or waterfall feature in the backyard. Add leaves from local trees and wildflowers to create a heartwarming rustic memorial.

There are many options for food in the great outdoors. Select paper goods that may be composted. For a hiking theme, serve trail mix, dried fruit, cheese and crackers, and fresh water. Some may prefer a lively barbecue with a fish fry, chips, salads and fresh fruit.

For music, the player should be loud enough that people can hear the songs but not so loud that it obscures the vital sounds of nature all around. Consider including the sounds of a river or paddles on a lake mixed in with a handful of the favorite songs of the person being remembered.

Families should give plenty of time to share fond memories and engage in discussion about their grief. This is one of the most fundamental reasons for the memorial service. In time, the ceremony itself becomes a beautiful memory for those who must come to grips with their loss.

PRACTICAL CONSIDERATIONS FOR BEACH/SEASIDE CEREMONIES

When it comes to the scattering or burial of ashes at sea, there are a few legal considerations hosts must research. Families who wish to include the scattering or burial of ashes in the water as part of the ceremony should make sure they follow local laws. Some states permit the scattering of ashes by plane, assuming the pilot has the proper permits and maintains a minimum altitude.

EPA regulations dictate that those who want to bury ashes in a permanent container must travel by boat three nautical miles from shore. In the state of California, those who wish to scatter ashes near a beach must go at least 500 yards from shore. Those ashes must be scattered without a container or using a container that sinks and dissolves within a few hours.

Hosting a memorial service at the beach presents some unique concerns. Consider the weather, proper seating, the best way to serve food and drink to guests, and general protection from the elements.

Tables and chairs can be tricky to set up, since they may sink into the sand or topple. To minimize this problem, use chairs and tables with wide feet. There are aftermarket products available to meet this need.

Canopies and awnings are easily available for rental or purchase to protect sensitive people and shield food items from the hot sun and wind. Check the timing of the tides, so the setup does not have to be moved to accommodate rising waters.

Planning for a beach ceremony may require some research into the best location for the event. Focus on the places the deceased loved to visit. Take into account accessibility for those with limited mobility, as well as travel distances to the beach. Memorial services are designed for friends and family to gather and grieve. Help make it easier for attendees by designing a local service or a short travel distance.

The ceremony planners might give themselves an hour or two to reminisce about their loved one and shared beach memories. Lazy evening barbecues and wonderful times spent with friends and family can become the focus of the ceremony.

During the ceremony, families can take advantage of the free nature of the beach. The best way to celebrate the deceased person's life might be a casual circle of friends talking about their favorite memories while they sit around a bonfire and watch the sunset. Or they could incorporate a more formal ceremony with a religious service and music.

Keep decorations simple and practical. Beaches are sandy and windy. Consider creating a display of beach photos next to the guest book registry. Add beach mementos such as driftwood, shells, rocks or beach glass. Dried flowers combined with dried greenery and driftwood make a unique arrangement that lasts a long time and creates an engaging talking point for guests. Beach-themed paper goods and decorations are fairly easy to find at specialty stores year-round.

For food, a beach picnic, barbecue or luau is a delightful choice. Sandwiches, fruit, grilled meat and desserts that are easy to eat by hand (such as cookies) are easy to serve, fun to eat and reasonably simple to clean up. For music, put together a mix CD of the deceased's favorite songs and familiar beach-related melodies to make a pleasant atmosphere that sparks cheerful memories.

CREMATION CEREMONY TEMPLATES

"Simple" is one popular reason people cite for choosing cremation. Simply send the body off to the crematory for direct cremation, and you don't have to mess with a funeral. No muss, no fuss — just deal with it, go home, and move on.

While that may sound good to those who want to avoid the messiness of mourning, this simple efficiency can leave a deep emotional hole to fill. Those who opt for direct cremation may not recognize the importance of some sort of goodbye ritual.

When a person is loved — or hated — that individual's passing really matters. The significance of the person's life calls for recognition. Without some sort of ritual to say goodbye to those who have died, death can generate an emotional black hole for the deceased's family and friends.

Grief counselors cite clinical experiences with patients who do not recognize a death with some sort of ceremony. Very often, six months later, these people seek professional help to process their grief.

Regardless of the disposition method, we humans need to express our emotions concerning a loss. Mourning at the time of death can prevent repression and psychological trouble down the road.

There are many ways to accomplish a good goodbye. The current trend is to celebrate the person's life, avoiding the somber trappings of a traditional funeral, memorial service, visitation and viewing. However the life is remembered, it's important to express emotions over the loss and receive the support of one's community.

VISITATIONS AND VIEWINGS

When a family chooses cremation for economic reasons, very often visitations and viewings get omitted because of the costs they add when working with a funeral home. But just because someone is going to be cremated doesn't mean there can't be a visitation with the family and/or a viewing of the deceased prior to the memorial service, if that's the family's custom. For little or no added cost, families can host their own visitations and can even hold viewings when they have a home-based funeral.

Visitation – Prior to a funeral or memorial service, family members receive support from their community at a visitation. Visitation provides time for the family to receive visitors who want to offer their condolences. It's a time to share stories and catch up with long-lost friends and relatives prior to a memorial service. This can be a day or two before the service or immediately before the funeral or cremation.

To help lighten the atmosphere, play a soundtrack of the deceased's favorite music, or play popular tunes appropriate to the age of the deceased. This is also a time for socializing. It is appropriate to have food and drink available. Visitation can take place at a funeral home, which can add to the overall funeral costs, or in a private residence.

Visitations are customary among people of Christian denominations. Members of the Jewish and Muslim faiths focus on burying the dead quickly and receiving community support after the funeral. Jewish mourners "sit shiva" at home for up to seven days after the funeral, with visitors welcome during this time. Muslims may observe up to 40 days of mourning at home after a death.

Viewing – The body of the deceased may be displayed for visitors to view as part of the visitation or funeral prior to cremation. Viewing is a highly individual choice for families, and it's not for everyone. In accordance with their traditions, Jews and Muslims generally do not host a public viewing of the body.

Some people are highly visual or touch-oriented. If they don't see the deceased actually laid out dead or have the opportunity to touch the body, they may not fully accept the reality of the death.

Embalming is not required by any state law. However, many funeral homes insist on embalming for any viewing involving people beyond immediate family or for a time span longer than 30 minutes. It is often the funeral home's own rules regarding viewings that are cited as the requirement for embalming.

If a person is going to be cremated, refrigeration is sufficient for preserving the body for a few days. Embalming is traditionally prohibited by the Jewish and Muslim faiths.

When cremation is to follow, the deceased may lie in a simple wooden casket or a more elaborate rental casket, or the body can simply be laid out on a bed, recliner or bier. If there is no casket, or if a rental casket is used, the body will be transferred into another container prior to cremation. Such containers are typically simple cardboard boxes that are used to place the body in the cremation retort.

TRADITIONAL VERSUS CELEBRANT-LED SERVICES

According to a 2015 study by the Pew Research Center's Forum on Religion and Public Life, 56 million people in the United States — and one-third of all adults under the age of 30 — have no religious affiliation, and their numbers are growing. Americans who choose "none" as their religious affiliation are the second largest religious group after evangelicals. "Nones" are affected when a death occurs and they don't know what to do for a funeral or memorial service.

In addition to the "nones," there are those who haven't been to religious services in years and feel uncomfortable around members of the clergy. But when Mom or Dad dies, they feel may feel the need to have a religious official do a traditional funeral service. Unfortunately, this kind of "cookie-cutter" service could be a funeral for anyone, which doesn't help family and friends process their grief.

Grief is a serious emotion that can drive wedges into loving relationships. People grieve over many kinds of losses — not only the death of people and pets but also changes in jobs, mental and physical declines, and friendships ending. Grief doesn't just go away; it needs to be recognized and addressed. If you've ever watched any of those television shows about hoarders, almost every case starts with a death in the family or another traumatic event.

A life celebration party with no mention of death does not help those who have lost a loved one. People need permission to grieve and a safe place to do it. Yes, a memorial service can be upbeat, but we also need the space and time to shed some tears over the loss and appreciate the significance of the death.

A memorial service helps people recognize their pain from the loss. It also helps establish the significance of the departed person's life, as so often we don't recognize what we've had until it's gone. And it helps people to recognize the impact that the deceased had in the wider community, allowing the community to mourn and celebrate with the family.

Ceremony and ritual speak for us when we don't know what to say. Involvement by those closest to the deceased, including preparing elements of the memorial service and participating in the ritual, is especially important. Creating a photomontage, providing a reading, selecting or playing music, and lighting candles are a few examples of ways people can participate and contribute.

A growing number of "spiritual but not religious" families are turning to funeral celebrants to create meaningful memorial services. Celebrants are trained to meet the needs of families during their time of loss by creating personalized memorial services that reflect the personalities and lifestyles of the deceased. Regardless of the family's beliefs or value system, celebrants leave their own religious leanings out of the discussion.

Celebrants meet with the family, listen to their stories about the deceased, discuss what was important to the person, and learn about the impact of his or her life. Based on this family meeting, which provides the opportunity for the healing of grief to start, the celebrant formulates the elements of the memorial service — the setting, the eulogy, the readings and music, ritual participation, other speakers, and a memorial takeaway gift for all attendees.

In some cases, the celebrant and the funeral director will both be involved with a memorial service at a funeral home. Alternatively, a family can work directly with a celebrant to construct a meaningful service after cremation has taken place.

The civil celebrant movement started in Australia in 1973. The Anglican and Roman Catholic Church liturgy wasn't working for the general population, especially those who were divorced. The government started licensing celebrants — non-clerics who could perform weddings and funerals outside of a religious ceremony. The movement recognized that nonbelievers and secular people have a place of equal respect in society.

Doug Manning, a former Baptist minister, brought the celebrant concept to the United States in 1999. He founded the In-Sight Institute to train and certify funeral celebrants. The institute provides a listing of trained celebrants at www.InSightBooks.com.

In the rest of this chapter, you will find templates for creating a variety of memorial services, including an extensive memorial service, a short memorial service, a nondenominational Christian service and a Jewish service. You'll find suggestions for additional readings and music in chapter 6.

Everyone deserves a good goodbye. Use these templates as a way to craft an individualized ritual for those who choose cremation.

FUNERAL/MEMORIAL SERVICE TEMPLATE

Here is an outline of a memorial service ceremony for someone who has been cremated. This ceremony template incorporates the four R's of a good goodbye:

- Recognize the death
- Remember the person
- Reaffirm beliefs
- Release the spirit of the deceased

This service template can be used for a variety of memorial services with or without cremated remains, as an outline for a private gathering for immediate family at home, for traditional or informal ceremonies, and at ash-scattering events. Those who opt to do their own home funerals can incorporate these elements as part of their rituals prior to cremation.

The service can be as upbeat and secular or as religious and somber as the family wants. If it's a secular service, a celebrant, the funeral director or a member of the family who is comfortable with public speaking can serve as the master or mistress of ceremonies. If the funeral is religious, a clergy person, preferably one who already knows the family, can preside over the service.

Components of the funeral or memorial service can include:

- Playing up to three meaningful pieces of music — one at the beginning, one in the middle, and one at the end of the service — either recorded or performed live by musicians.
- Welcoming attendees to the service and focusing on the significance of the event.
- Reminding everyone present to silence or turn off electronic devices to maintain a sacred space for the service.
- Introducing the person who lived and died. An obituary is often read to provide an overview of the person's life, or the celebrant can prepare a life story or eulogy.
- Telling stories about the deceased that share details about his or her life, death, values, passions and accomplishments. These stories can come from prepared eulogies by those close to the deceased; further stories may come from the celebrant and/or open comments from attendees.
- Showing a video montage of photos set to music featuring the deceased with family and friends.

Stating beliefs about life, death and the afterlife — whatever the family believes to be true — is the third R: reaffirming beliefs. This can be a tricky line to navigate, as members of a family may hold divergent beliefs, from atheistic to evangelical. The reading below by Benjamin

Franklin provides a possible middle ground.

For those families who would appreciate Bible readings, the 23rd Psalm ("The Lord is my shepherd; I shall not want ..."), the 121st Psalm ("I lift my eyes to the mountains ...") and Ecclesiastes 3:1 ("To everything there is a season ...") can provide a measure of comfort.

Closing with a statement that sends the deceased on his or her way to whatever comes next and the living to their new lives without the deceased provides the fourth R: release. Here's a closing statement you may use:

> While _____ is no longer present in physical form, he/she will live on in the hearts and minds of those present — and by carrying _____ in our memory, he/she becomes immortal. Let us resolve to go forth from today's service inspired to live better lives thanks to _____ 's example and dedicate ourselves to the higher causes that _____ held dear.

—Celebrant Gail Rubin, CT

Benjamin Franklin's Words

Here is a lovely reading for the third R, reaffirming beliefs, that is appropriate for almost any funeral, save for those including staunch atheists and certain humanists. These words were written by Benjamin Franklin:

> We are spirits. That bodies should be lent us, while they can afford us pleasure, assist us in acquiring knowledge, or in doing good to our fellow creatures, is a kind and benevolent act of God — when they become unfit for these purposes and afford us pain instead of pleasure — instead of an aid, become an encumbrance and answer none of the intentions for which they were given, it is equally kind and benevolent that a way is provided by which we may get rid of them. Death is that way....

Our friend and we are invited abroad on a party of pleasure — that is to last forever. His chair was ready first and he is gone before us. We could not all conveniently start together, and why should you and I be grieved at this, since we are soon to follow, and we know where to find him.

—*Benjamin Franklin*

Cremation Ceremony

Chapels that incorporate a retort are common in Great Britain, but they are not yet widespread in the United States. In a cremation chapel, at a funeral's end, the casket is slowly lowered out of sight or curtains are closed before the casket moves into the retort.

If the funeral home has a chapel connected to the cremation retort, the beginning of the cremation process can make a moving end to the funeral. However, many cremation retorts are located in industrial settings. This makes a ceremonial transition to the cremation problematic. Those closest to the deceased might go to the retort for the final disposition.

Whether in a chapel or an industrial setting, a designated family member or friend can push the button to start the cremation process. A reading or prayer may be said at this time.

This statement for reciting at the start of a cremation can help with the fourth R, release:

_____, we consign your body to the flames, consuming your physical body and releasing your spirit. We remember all the good you brought to this life and forgive your faults. As you pass from this physical lifetime, we wonder where we go after breath has left our bodies. Your memory burns brightly in our hearts, and as long as we remember you, you will live on. Go your way in peace.

—*Celebrant Gail Rubin, CT*

SHORT MEMORIAL SERVICE TEMPLATE

Sometimes, a long, drawn-out memorial service isn't needed, but you still want to say something about the deceased. Here's a structure for a short but meaningful service that covers the four R's of a good memorial service: recognizing the death, remembering the person, reaffirming beliefs and releasing the spirit.

Feel free to add readings and play music that reflects the spirit of the person who died to add depth and emotional impact to the service.

Recognize

The service begins with a brief introduction. For example:

> We are assembled here today to pay respects to our honored dead — to remember the life and mark the death of _____. He/she had an impact on all of us, so we take this brief time to recognize his/her death. He/she was ___ years old when (manner of death) took him/her from our midst.
>
> _____ would not have wanted us to make a big fuss, and so we'll keep our observance today short and sweet.

Remember

Next, list three to five words that describe the deceased, and then tell a short story about why each word is a potent descriptor of the deceased and his/her character. For example:

> These words describe (*name*): (*word 1*), (*word 2*) and (*word 3*).
>
> *Short stories follow.*

Reaffirm

Following the remembrance portion of the service, it is helpful to reaffirm the beliefs of those in attendance. Here is a suggested way to do just that:

The theologian William Barclay said, "When I die, I should like to slip out of the room without fuss — for what matters is not what I am leaving, but where I am going." _____ knew what mattered in life, and he/she has left us to remember what matters after his/her death.

If appropriate for the beliefs of those gathered:

The soul or spirit sheds its earthly body as a tree sheds its leaves and creates for itself another covering, in another sphere, as the tree grows new leaves. Death is not the end of existence but merely the cessation of the earthly phase of life. It is a corner we turn to reach a perfect, peaceful spiritual life.

As the Beatles so eloquently sang, "All you need is love." Let us extend our love for _____ in our daily interactions, for by keeping his/her love alive in our hearts, he/she will never truly die.

Release

Lastly, it is time to release the spirit of the departed. Here is one way to do so:

_____, we bless your memory with great love for you, for you have written your love upon our hearts. Go your way in peace, and may your memory be a blessing to all who knew you.

If appropriate, you might raise a toast:

To the life and adventures of _____ !

This short, informal memorial service can precede a scattering ceremony for cremated remains. After the service, socializing with food and drink is a great way to share additional stories and memories about the deceased.

A Nondenominational Christian Memorial Service

Those who have a Christian background but aren't currently associated with a particular church may want to utilize this memorial service outline for the traditional passages that it offers. Those who belong to a church may want to rely on a familiar clergy person to create a meaningful Christian service.

Most funeral homes have contacts with freelance ministers who can fulfill the role of clergy person. A celebrant can also utilize this service template and adjust it to your family's individual preferences.

The singing of hymns or the playing of recorded songs may be inserted almost anyplace throughout the service. It's recommended to incorporate two or three hymns or songs at most.

Invocation

SPEAKER: In the name of the Father and the Son and the Holy Spirit.

CONGREGATION: Amen.

SPEAKER: Blessed be the God and Father of our Lord Jesus Christ, the source of all mercy and the God of all consolation. He comforts us in all our sorrows so that we can comfort others in their sorrows with the consolation we ourselves have received from God.

CONGREGATION: Thanks be to God.

Prayer

The following prayer may be offered by the officiant:

O Lord, we are here today with thoughts of life and death on our minds. We seek your help as we struggle with our feelings, our thoughts, our doubts and fears, and our confident faith in you and your promises. Give us comfort during this hour, and with the passing of time, turn our sorrow at this death to rejoicing at the new life you have given your servant, _____.

As we who are left face life each day, give us hope and wisdom that, trusting in you to guide us, we may finally come to the place you have prepared for those who die in faith, where we will be at home with you and those who have gone before us in eternal joy and celebration, through Jesus Christ, our Lord. Amen.

The Obituary

This is an opportunity to read a newspaper obituary prepared by the family or an overview of the person's life prepared by the celebrant or clergy person.

Scripture Lessons

The following scripture lessons are particularly applicable to memorial services.

Isaiah 35:5-7 and 40:31

SPEAKER: The prophet Isaiah, writing of a better time to come — the time when the Lord himself would come to deliver his people — described that time in these words:

Then the eyes of the blind shall be opened and the ears of the deaf unstopped;
Then shall the lame man leap like a deer and the tongue of the speechless sing for joy.
For waters shall break forth in the wilderness and streams in the desert;
The burning sand shall become a pool and the thirsty ground springs of water.

Those who wait for the Lord shall renew their strength;
They shall mount up with wings like eagles;
They shall run and not be weary;
They shall walk and not faint.

1 Corinthians 15:35-44

SPEAKER: St. Paul, in his rather direct way, wrote a letter to people who were concerned with death and dying and with the resurrection of the body. This is what he had to say:

But someone will ask, "How are the dead raised? With what kind of body do they come?" You foolish man! What you sow does not come to life unless it dies, and what you sow is not the body that is to be, but a bare kernel, perhaps of wheat or some other grain. But God gives it a body as He has chosen, and to each kind of seed its own body....

So it is with the resurrection of the dead. What is sown is perishable; what is raised is imperishable. It is sown in dishonor; it is raised in glory. It is sown in weakness; it is raised in power. It is sown in a physical body; it is raised in a spiritual body.

Address

Following the scripture lesson, the officiant will typically give an address. Here is a sample that can be used or adapted as needed:

Life is often compared to a journey. We have all come from some place and are headed for another. Our stay here is quite brief, compared with eternity. Yet momentous things happen during our few years on earth.

When blessed with a long life, we have the opportunity to have an impact on many people. It is difficult, if not impossible, to measure the influence a man/woman has on his/her family, friends and those with whom he/she works, but we know that influence can be considerable. Today we give thanks for the way _____'s family and friends were influenced by his/her life. This is a time of thanksgiving.

Death is seen sometimes only as a tragedy. Indeed, we spend much time, energy and effort avoiding death. Yet by God's grace, death has become the entrance of the faithful into eternal life.

While today is a time to mourn and to express our grief at this loss, it is also a time to celebrate _____'s new life — a life without pain, without the limitations of illness or injury. His/Her new life is life in a new body, a restored healthy body, without the frailty, pain and sadness we experience in this world.

Indeed, it occurs to us at times that life as we know it on earth is not always preferable to death, since God in his own way has changed the very nature of death so that, instead of doing us harm, it has become our entrance to another life that is so far superior to this one that words fail to describe it.

The 23rd Psalm

Invite attendees to join in the recitation.

> The Lord is my shepherd; I shall not want.
> He makes me to lie down in green pastures;
> He leads me beside the still waters.
> He restores my soul.
> He guides me in straight paths for His Name's sake.

Yea, though I walk through the valley of the shadow of death,
I will fear no evil, for Thou art with me.
Thy rod and Thy staff — they comfort me.
Thou preparest a table before me in the presence of mine enemies;
Thou annointest my head with oil;
My cup runneth over.
Surely goodness and mercy shall follow me all the days of my life;
And I shall dwell in the house of the Lord forever.

Commendation Prayer

The commendation prayer is a way of thanking God for the opportunity to have loved the deceased and for returning the deceased to God's care.

O God of grace and glory, we remember before you today our brother/sister, _____. We thank you for giving him/her to us to know and to love as a companion in our pilgrimage on earth.

Holy God, by your creative power, you gave us life, and in your redeeming love you have given us new life in Christ. We commend _____ to your merciful care in the faith of Christ, our Lord, who died and rose again to save us and who now lives and reigns with you and the Holy Spirit, one God, now and forever.

In your boundless compassion, console us who mourn. Give us your aid, so we may see in death the gate to eternal life, that we may continue our course on earth in confidence until, by your call, we are reunited with those who have gone before us, through your Son, Jesus Christ, our Lord. Amen.

The Lord's Prayer

The Lord's Prayer is a well-known ritual prayer that many people find comforting in times of loss.

> Our Father, who art in heaven, hallowed be thy name.
> Thy kingdom come, thy will be done, on earth as it is in heaven.
> Give us this day our daily bread and forgive us our debts, as we forgive our debtors.
> And lead us not into temptation, but deliver us from evil.
> For thine is the kingdom, and the power, and the glory, forever. Amen.

Benediction

The benediction is the concluding prayer of the service.

> SPEAKER: The Lord bless us, defend us from all evil, and bring us to everlasting life.
>
> CONGREGATION: Amen.
>
> SPEAKER: God of all mercies and giver of all comfort, look graciously, we pray, on those who mourn, that, casting all their care on you, they may know the consolation of your love, through Jesus Christ, our Lord.
>
> CONGREGATION: Amen.

Following the benediction, the officiant should announce any post-ceremony gatherings.

JEWISH MEMORIAL SERVICE TEMPLATE

Jewish funeral services are generally very short. Whether held in a funeral home, a synagogue, at graveside or in other places, Jewish funerals, at their most basic, are comprised of a eulogy that says truthful things about the deceased, the prayer *El Malei Rachamim* ("Source of Compassion") and, once the deceased's body or cremated remains are in the grave, the Mourner's *Kaddish*.

The following psalms and readings can help fill out a Jewish funeral service. Feel free to pick those readings that resonate with you.

Psalm 121

I lift my eyes to the mountains (or hills) — from where will my help come?
My help comes from God, who made heaven and earth.
God will not allow your foot to stumble; God who keeps you will not slumber.
Behold, the Guardian of Israel neither slumbers nor sleeps.
The Eternal is your keeper; God is your shade at your right hand.
The sun shall not strike you by day, nor the moon by night.
God shall preserve you from all evil; the Eternal shall preserve your soul.
God shall preserve your going out and your coming in from this time forth and forevermore.

Psalm 15

Lord, who may abide in Your House?
Who may dwell in Your holy mountain?
Those who are upright; who do justly; who speak the truth within their hearts.
Who do not slander others, or wrong them, or bring shame upon them.
Who scorn the lawless, but honor those who revere God.
Who give their word and, come what may, do not retract.
Who do not exploit others; who do not take bribes.
Those who live in this way shall never be shaken.

Psalm 90

O God, You have been our refuge in every generation.
Before the mountains came into being,
Before You brought forth the earth and the world,
From eternity to eternity, You are God.
You return us to dust;
You decreed: "Return, you mortals!"
For in Your sight a thousand years are as yesterday when it
has passed,
As a watch in the night.
You engulf us in sleep; we are like grass that renews itself;
At daybreak it flourishes anew;
At dusk it withers and dries up.
The span of our life is threescore years and ten, or, given
strength, fourscore years;
But the best of those years have trouble and sorrow.
They pass by speedily, and we are in darkness.
Teach us, therefore, so to number our days that we may at-
tain a heart of wisdom.
Turn to us, O God!
Show mercy to Your servants.
Satisfy us at daybreak with Your steadfast love that we may
sing for joy all our days.
Let Your deeds be seen by Your servants, Your glory by their
children.
May Your favor, O God, be upon us.
Establish the work of our hands that it may long endure.

Additional Readings

The following passages, found in the "Rabbi's Manual" from the
Central Conference of American Rabbis and other Jewish prayer books,
are often included in Jewish memorial services:

God, You give us loved ones and make them the strength of

our life, the light of our eyes. They depart and leave us bereft on a lonely way, but You are the living fountain from which our healing flows. To You the stricken look for comfort, and the sorrow-laden for consolation.

O God, we see life as through windows that open on eternity. We see that love endures and the soul endures, as You, O God, endure forever. We see that the years are more than grass that withers, more than flowers that fade. They weave a timeless pattern in a world that is the dwelling place of Your love and glory.

In nature's ebb and flow, God's eternal law abides. When tears dim our vision and grief clouds our understanding, we often lose sight of God's eternal plan. Yet we know that growth and decay, life and death, all reveal the divine purpose. God, who is our support in the struggles of life, is also our hope in death. We have set God before us and shall not despair. In God's hands are the souls of the living and the spirits of all flesh. Under divine protection we abide, and by God's love we are comforted. O Life of our life, Soul of our soul, cause Your light to shine into our hearts, and fill our spirit with abiding trust in You.

May the memory of _____ endure among us as a blessing. In Your own time, O God, when we too are called to enter eternity, may we leave this life secure in the faith that in Your light we shall see light. In life and in death, we cannot go where You are not, and where You are, hope endures. Sustained by this assurance, we invoke Your name, Almighty God.

O God of life, amid the ceaseless tides of change that sweep away the generations, Your love remains to comfort us and to give us hope. Around us are life and death, decay and renewal: the flowing rhythm that all things obey.

Our life is a dance to a song we cannot hear. Its melody courses through us for a little while, then seems to cease. Whence the melody, and whither does it go? In darkness as in light, we turn to You, the source of life, and the answer to all its mysteries.

Early or late, all must answer the summons to return to the Source of being, for we lose our hold on life when our time has come, as the leaf falls from the bough when its day is done. The deeds of the righteous enrich us all, as the fallen leaf enriches the soil beneath. The dust returns to the earth; the spirit lives on with God.

Like the stars by day, our beloved dead are not seen by mortal eyes. They shine on forever; theirs is eternal peace.

Psalm 23; A Psalm of David

The Lord is my shepherd; I shall not want.
He makes me to lie down in green pastures;
He leads me beside the still waters.
He restores my soul.
He guides me in straight paths for His Name's sake.
Yea, though I walk through the valley of the shadow of death,
I will fear no evil, for Thou art with me.
Thy rod and Thy staff — they comfort me.
Thou preparest a table before me in the presence of mine enemies;
Thou annointest my head with oil;
My cup runneth over.

Surely goodness and mercy shall follow me all the days of my life;
And I shall dwell in the house of the Lord forever.

El Malei Rachamim (Source of Compassion)

Merciful God, God Most High, let there be perfect rest for the souls of our loved ones who have gone into eternity. May they find shelter in Your presence among the holy and pure whose light shines like the radiance of heaven. May their souls be bound up in the bond of life eternal. May they find a home in You. And may they rest in peace. Together we say: Amen.

Mourner's *Kaddish*

The Mourner's *Kaddish* is traditionally recited at Jewish funerals. First, we provide the Hebrew transliteration. The English translation follows.

Hebrew:

Yit'gadal v'yit'kadash sh'mei raba

CONGREGATION: Amen.

B'al'ma di v'ra khir'utei
V'yam'likh mal'khutei b'chayeikhon uv'yomeikhon
Uv'chayei d'khol beit yis'ra'eil
Ba'agala uviz'man kariv v'im'ru:

CONGREGATION: Amen.

Y'hei sh'mei raba m'varakh l'alam ul'al'mei al'maya
Yit'barakh v'yish'tabach v'yit'pa'ar v'yit'romam v'yit'nasei
V'yit'hadar v'yit'aleh v'yit'halal sh'mei d'kud'sha

CONGREATION: B'rikh hu.

L'eila min kol bir'khata v'shirata
toosh'b'chatah v'nechematah, da'ameeran b'al'mah,
v'eemru:

CONGREGATION: Amen.

Y'hei sh'lama raba min sh'maya
V'chayim aleinu v'al kol yis'ra'eil v'im'ru:

CONGREGATION: Amen.

Oseh shalom bim'romav hu ya'aseh shalom
Aleinu v'al kol Yis'ra'eil v'im'ru:

CONGREGATION: Amen.

English:

Let the glory of God be extolled. Let His great name be hallowed in the world whose creation He willed. May His kingdom soon prevail, in our own day, our own lives, and the life of all Israel, and let us say:

CONGREGATION: Amen.

Let His great name be blessed forever and ever.
Let the name of the Holy One —

CONGREGATION: Blessed is He.

— be glorified, exalted and honored, though He is beyond all the praises, songs and adorations that we can utter, and let us say:

CONGREGATION: Amen.

For us and for all Israel, may the blessing of peace and the promise of life come true, and let us say:

CONGREGATION: Amen.

May He who causes peace to reign in the high heavens, let peace descend on us, on all Israel, and all the world, and let us say:

CONGREGATION: Amen.

May the Source of peace send peace to all who mourn and comfort to all who are bereaved, and let us say:

CONGREGATION: Amen.

Conclusion

The service concludes with a brief prayer:

Let us be thankful for the companionship that continues in a love stronger than death. Sanctifying the name of God, we honor the memory of _____. Go your way, for God has called you.

CONGREGATION (to the family/mourners): May God comfort you among the mourners of Zion and Jerusalem.

Optionally, the officiant may then say to the attendees:

Please form two rows for the family to pass through while leaving. This shows your support of the mourners as they journey from the grave to the next steps in their lives.

Then, make any announcements about post-ceremony gatherings.

Note: If the remains are being buried in a cemetery, traditionally, the memorial marker is not set until a year has passed. The family returns for the unveiling of the marker near the anniversary of the death; this is usually a small ceremonial gathering.

Post-Ceremony

After any type of funeral or cremation service, attendees may gather for further storytelling and to share support over food and drink. This gathering can take place at the funeral home, at a restaurant, in a private residence, or in a meaningful indoor or outdoor setting.

5

SAMPLE CELEBRANT SCRIPTS

These three scripts provide concrete examples of services that were held for actual people. Their families granted permission to share these service scripts here.

FUNERAL FOR HY WARREN

This service was created for a family that came from Jewish roots but was raised without any Jewish religious observance. The family wanted the traditions of a Jewish funeral without any mention of God.

At the funeral home, there was a brief viewing of the deceased and a short ceremony before the family proceeded to the cemetery for a graveside service.

Keriah

We start our funeral ritual with a ribbon-tearing ceremony called *Keriah*. This originated with the Biblical story of the patriarch Jacob, when he was told that his favorite son, Joseph, had been killed by wild beasts. This was actually a lie told by his brothers, who had sold him off into slavery. Nonetheless, Jacob tore his clothing as an expression of his grief. We also see the rending of garments by Job, when told that his sons and daughters had all been killed.

The tearing of cloth gives physical expression to the emotions that we may be holding inside about the death of our loved one. As we start the funeral, this is the time to let those emotions flow. Rather than tear a perfectly good article of clothing, we have these ribbons to tear and pin to your clothing.

There is a prayer that you may say as you tear the ribbon: *Baruch atah Adonai, dayan ha-emet.* This means, "Blessed is the true judge."

Children wear the ribbon on the left side for a parent. Others may wear the ribbon on the right side.

Travel to cemetery for 1:00 graveside service. Family follows hearse in limo.

Placement of casket and flag, accompanied by classical music.

Greeting and Introduction

Voltaire said, "Let us read and let us dance — two amusements that will never do any harm to the world." Hy Warren loved both reading and dancing. In his honor, please turn off your cell phones or electronic devices, so we can keep this ceremony a sacred time in this sacred place and focus fully on what we are about to do.

In Shakespeare's play, "As You Like It," we find these lines:

All the world's a stage,
And all the men and women merely players;
They have their exits and their entrances,
And one man in his time plays many parts,
His acts being seven ages.

Hy Warren loved the theater, and he has reached the final act of his time upon this worldly stage.

We are here to support each other at this time of life transition. We are here for Hy's sons, Richard and Robert;

for Richard's wife, Judy Zabel; and grandchildren Adam, Jennifer and Jenny. We keep in our hearts Hy's late wife, Ellie; infant son, Jodi; and late companion, Florence. Our human connections help us to bear the grief that we feel today.

Welcome. My name is Gail Rubin, and I am honored to be the funeral celebrant for today's service. We gather today to remember and celebrate the life of Hy "Schotz" or "Schotzie" Warren. That's Polish or German for "sweetheart." And what a sweetheart he was.

Gregarious, stubborn and funny are three words that describe Hy Warren. He was that and so much more.

Hy was born Hyman Warshawsky on August 9, 1918, in Patterson, New Jersey. He was a first generation American born to parents who had fled Russia at the turn of the 20th century. He had a sister, Dora, and a brother, Leo. The family moved to New York, and Hy lived in the North Bronx neighborhoods of Allerton Avenue and Pelham Park for 70 years. It was a big Jewish neighborhood, and ever since he was little, he had the nickname Schotz.

As a child in the 1920s and 1930s, Hy was involved with "The Coops," a cooperative of Jewish socialists who marched on May Day and were involved in other activities year-round. Hy was a member of the Young Pioneers, a Socialist version of the Boy Scouts, a time he remembered as some of the best days of his life.

While he later recanted his views on socialism, he enjoyed running into "coopniks" from New York after he moved to Florida.

Hy graduated from Evander Childs High School in 1936, in the depths of the Great Depression. While he did not finish college, he relished reading and learning throughout his life. He especially loved reading about the U.S. Civil War and other wars throughout time.

At the age of 18, while living in the Bronx, Hy met Elenor, or Ellie, who was 15 at the time. Their love bloomed and lasted through 55 years of marriage. Their favorite date was going to the theater and having dinner at a Chinese restaurant — and of course, dancing. Hy liked nothing better than dancing up a storm. His family even gave him the moniker of "Last Man Dancing."

As a young man and throughout his life, Hy loved attending theater productions. Before World War II, he had a huge collection of playbills from productions he had seen in New York City over 10 to 15 years. Unfortunately, his father threw out the playbill collection while he was away during the war.

Hy started a small commercial printing business in the Bronx. When the U.S. got involved in World War II, Hy joined the Navy and trained to be a pharmacist's mate, essentially a medic. However, when the military saw in his paperwork that he was a printer by trade, they changed his assignment.

The military needed printers to produce manuals and other materials, so Hy spent the war years in Washington, D.C., printing. He got to eat steak and ice cream and gained 35 pounds during his time there. After he got out of the Navy, he shortened his last name to Warren.

After running his printing business for many years, and having Richard work with him, Hy and son Rob and Ellie opened a card store and bookshop called Ellie's Place. The family worked together for 10 years, until the business was sold and the couple retired to Florida 20 years ago.

Hy, ever the social one, became a telemarketer while living in Coconut Creek, near Fort Lauderdale. He'd sell septic tank cleaning, despite not knowing anything about septic tanks. He also sold gold and other goods and services. And he was really good at it!

In New York, he was a baseball fan of the Brooklyn Dodgers. After moving to Florida, he rooted for the Miami teams in all sports. And he played a mean game of the family's own Full Contact Jewish Dishes. Just the mention of Moishe Pipick would make him laugh.

Hy loved good food and drink — and any kind of chocolate. He is legendary for his statement, "Coke with the meal." He had no patience for wait staff who would bring the soda early, before the food arrived and before free refills were common. "Coke WITH the meal."

Ellie died 15 years ago. After a few years of mourning, Hy and Florence got together. They shared a number of good years together until Florence died unexpectedly. Hy started a relationship with Sally, and then Richard moved Hy here to New Mexico to better care for him. The long span of years had begun to take a toll on this robust man.

Adam provided these comments to Grandpa Hy:

> When I was just around six or seven years old, I went to New York to see you and Grandma. I remember getting off that plane and how you treated me as if I were the prince of New York itself. I remember how sad and homesick I was when I first arrived and how you made it all better for me. Before the end of the trip, I didn't want to go back home.
>
> Grandpa, you will always be that strong and stern man

who never let go 'til the very end. You had the strength and wisdom that so few others had. You always made me laugh and smile. You had the fortitude of an ox and the stubbornness to go along with it. Thank you for teaching me and guiding me through my life.

You will be missed, Grandpa. "To the world, you were somebody, but to me you were the world."

Love,
Adam

He was funny, sweet, lovable — and sometimes, a royal pain in the butt. He said what was on his mind and could be very stubborn. His sense of humor was with him to the end.

Richard and Jennifer were with him when he drew his last breath. He went gently into that good night.

Ecclesiastes and Comments

From the book of Ecclesiastes we learn:

To everything there is a season,
A time for every purpose under the sun.
A time to be born and a time to die;
A time to plant and a time to pluck up that which is planted;
A time to kill and a time to heal ...
A time to weep and a time to laugh;
A time to mourn and a time to dance ...
A time to embrace and a time to refrain from embracing;
A time to lose and a time to seek;
A time to rend and a time to sew;
A time to keep silent and a time to speak....

This is a time to speak. I invite you to tell your personal stories about Hy, that we may share both laughter and tears.

Open comments

Presentation of Flag

This American flag, which honors Hy's service in the Navy, will be presented to his grandson Adam, who served in the Air Force.

On behalf of the president of the United States and the chief of naval operations, please accept this flag as a symbol of our appreciation for your loved one's service to this country and a grateful Navy.

Meditation

Our life is a dance to a song we cannot hear. Its melody courses through us for a little while — then seems to cease. Whence the melody, and whither does it go?

Early or late, all must answer the summons to return to the source of being, for we lose our hold on life when our time has come, as the leaf falls from the bough when its day is done. The deeds of the righteous enrich us all, as the fallen leaf enriches the soil beneath. The dust returns to the earth; the spirit lives on in the hearts of those who remember.

Like the stars by day, our beloved dead are not seen by mortal eyes. They shine on forever. May they rest in eternal peace. Let us be thankful for the companionship that continues in a love stronger than death. We honor the memory of Hy Warren.

Lowering the Casket

The Jewish tradition of throwing earth on the casket is almost as well-known as the tradition of breaking a glass at a wedding. The sound of the earth on the casket is a visceral experience that truly drives home the reality that this loved one is dead.

You are invited to throw one or three shovelfuls of earth onto the casket. While one is sufficient, three shows intention of burying the dead. Replace the shovel in the earth, rather than passing it from hand to hand. The tradition is that pain should not be passed along.

After reciting the Mourner's *Kaddish*, as we depart, you'll see at the edge of the cemetery a pitcher of water and a basin. The tradition of washing the hands upon leaving the cemetery has origins that are both practical and ritual. If we were called upon to fill this grave ourselves, as families have done before professionals were hired to do the job, we would want to wash our hands at the end of the burial.

As a ritual, the washing of the hands is done because being in close proximity to the dead makes us ritually impure. We wash our hands to make ourselves spiritually clean, as well as physically.

Recitation of the Mourner's Kaddish in Hebrew.

Parting words

We stand here in sadness. We also stand here in gratitude. Hy lived a rich and a full life. May all who mourn today find comfort in the years that we were given. May we emulate Hy's positive life examples. May we find the vigor to enhance the life of others and be a blessing for all with whom we come in contact.

And as you leave today, you will be given a special memory

gift. Hy was known for his insistence on "Coke WITH the meal," not before. He was also a lover of chocolate.

Pull out Coke bottle.

Take one of these bottles and a chocolate heart with you. These serve as a remembrance of Hy and his love of food, laughter and life. When you eat the chocolate, remember Schotz as the sweet man that he was. I will hand one to each of you after you've had a chance to wash your hands.

As we go forth from this place, let us keep Hy's spirit in our hearts. May the source of peace send peace to all who mourn and comfort to all who are bereaved. Shalom.

Big Band music plays.

You can see a video of this service on YouTube at:
http://youtu.be/C_TaUDEKLbs.

MEMORIAL SERVICE FOR MARY ADAMS

Mary Adams planned her memorial service with her son and Celebrant Gail Rubin six months before she died. Among the elements discussed were the speakers, the readings, bagpipe music to be played by her nephew, and who to invite to the cocktail party after the memorial service. Her proactive planning made it so much easier to create this meaningful, memorable memorial service after her death.

First Corinthians 13: The Greatest Gift

Though I speak with the tongues of men and of angels, but have not love, I have become sounding brass or a clanging cymbal.

And though I have the gift of prophecy, and understand all mysteries and all knowledge, and though I have all faith, so that I could remove mountains, but have not love, I am nothing.

And though I bestow all my goods to feed the poor, and though I give my body to be burned, but have not love, it profits me nothing.

Love suffers long and is kind; love does not envy; love does not parade itself, is not puffed up; does not behave rudely, does not seek its own, is not provoked, thinks no evil; does not rejoice in iniquity, but rejoices in the truth; bears all things, believes all things, hopes all things, endures all things.

Love never fails. But whether there are prophecies, they will fail; whether there are tongues, they will cease; whether there is knowledge, it will vanish away. For we know in part and we prophesy in part. But when that which is perfect has come, then that which is in part will be done away.

When I was a child, I spoke as a child, I understood as a child, I thought as a child; but when I became an adult, I put away childish things. For now we see in a mirror, dimly, but then face to face. Now I know in part, but then I shall know just as I also am known.

And now abide faith, hope, love, these three; but the greatest of these is love.

Greeting and Commentary

Welcome. My name is Gail Rubin, and I am honored to be the celebrant for today's service honoring and remembering the life of Mary Adams.

Today, we speak with love about a woman who has touched our lives in so many ways. To avoid distractions of sounding brass or clanging cymbal, and to be fully present in our remembrance, please silence or turn off your cell phone or electronic devices for the duration of this service. Thank you.

It is an important day when we stop to bear witness to a person's life and times among us — the difference her living and dying made — and to reflect on our hope, our wonder and our collected grief. It is a time to create a circle of support for the loved ones gathered here.

On behalf of the family, thank you for being here for this important moment. We are here in support of Mary's son, Michael; her grandchildren, Devon, Gray, Ian and Kayla; Mary's sister, Jean; and her children, David, Doug, Andrew and Susan; and her husband, Jay.

Mary said that she wanted us to talk about her, not what she did. Yet so much of what she did is a reflection of who she was: a woman of many talents and interests, of intellect and activity.

Mary Adams, born Mary Elizabeth Atcheson, came from Irish stock. We all know how well the Irish weave a story. She always had a twinkle in her eye. She was always ready to strike a dancer's pose. Not only could Mary tell a good story, she wrote stories. She listened to stories of family, of friends and of clients. She edited stories. Her life was a story of grand proportions.

Mary said her family lineage in the United States stretched back to a forebear from Ireland who came to this continent and served in George Washington's army. He very wisely married a lieutenant's daughter, which brought added benefits.

Mary was born in Washington, Iowa. She came from a long line of farmers, the men, and teachers, the women. In the

1920s, when women got the right to vote, her mother told her she didn't have to be a teacher. She could be anything she wanted to be.

Well, Mary was a teacher, and she was so much more – a dancer, a reporter, an editor, an art curator, a publisher, a grant writer, a social worker, a clinical psychotherapist, an advocate for the underdog, a wife, a mother, a grandmother, a lover and a friend.

When Mary was a teenager, she spent a summer in Washington, D.C., and met Eleanor Roosevelt in person. If Mary wasn't already a liberal, she certainly was after that meeting. Throughout her life, she supported causes: the Southern Poverty Law Center, Doctors Without Borders, several veterans groups and Native American tribes.

Mary attended the University of California in Los Angeles. While pursuing her B.A. degree at UCLA, Mary was also active in dance and drama. One day, she was in the theater painting a set when Clinton Adams walked by. He said, "You're doing that wrong."

Thus started a romantic relationship and a professional partnership that lasted more than six decades. They married while Clinton was on leave during World War II, and she held jobs almost everywhere Clinton's career took them.

In the 1940s, when Clinton was in the Army Air Corps in Colorado Springs, Mary served as a corps administrative assistant. In the early '50s, they went back to Los Angeles, with Clinton at UCLA. Mary was an elementary school teacher, an assistant at UCLA and an assistant at the J. Paul Getty Museum in Malibu.

In the latter half of the '50s, while Clinton worked at the

University of Kentucky, Mary was a reporter for a radio station and for UPI, the United Press International wire service. They were in Gainesville, Florida, when Michael was born, and she took some time off to be a mom. There was another jaunt back to UCLA in the early '60s, and then the call came. Mary and Clinton arrived in Albuquerque for their long association with the University of New Mexico.

In 1962, Mary and Clinton moved into a stunning California contemporary home on Morningside Drive here in Albuquerque. In this home, she continued to work to improve the lives of the less fortunate. She wrote and published books and articles. And she became a counselor and psychotherapist at the age of 57.

She was a voracious news junkie. She was keenly interested in following and discussing politics, and she loved political satire. We're talking about the music of Tom Lehrer and TV programs such as "That Was the Week That Was," "Rowan and Martin's Laugh-In" and, most recently, "The Daily Show With Jon Stewart" and "Politically Incorrect With Bill Maher."

Always the consummate hostess, Mary expertly made introductions and connections between people at her gatherings. Her Winter Solstice parties are legendary. No matter the date, cocktails were served at 5 o'clock; hence, the timing of our remembrance here today.

Many famous artists visited Mary and Clinton's home, and art was all over the house. A Matisse hung in the bathroom. Georgia O'Keeffe was a friend, and Mary published several essays about her and other artists.

Mary lived in that home for 50 years. And on the sunny morning of March 8, at the age of 91, with son Michael and sister Jean by her side, she peacefully died there.

Mary was my next-door neighbor for the last 20 years. There's now a hole in my heart when I look at her house. Truly, love makes a house a home.

Mary was also a prolific list-maker and used yellow sticky notes extensively. Back in September, she asked me to come over to meet with her and Michael to plan this service. We laughed together as we sketched out her final party. What a gift this was. We knew how she wanted her life to be celebrated. Today, those plans are a reality.

We'll now hear stories about Mary from her sister, Jean Willson.

Jean Willson speaks.

One of the people that Mary wanted to speak here today was Jim Belshaw, the former Albuquerque Journal columnist who was a longtime friend of both she and Clinton. He was unable to attend due to a family commitment; however, he sent these words for me to share with you.

> Mary and I talked about a lot of things — politics, art, journalism, psychology. We talked about UNM and the city and the state. We talked about her history and mine. We talked about her FBI "sheet." I loved the strange irony of this beautiful woman, who was exactly the kind of American America needed, being looked at askance by the FBI. It made me think of all the times Tony Hillerman needled the FBI. I remember thinking that if the FBI thought it needed to investigate Mary Adams, then everything Hillerman said about them was right.

> Mary and I talked about Clinton and his art and what made him the artist he was. We talked about her writing

and mine. We went to lunch, or I came to the house, and we just let the conversation go wherever it wanted to go.

Regardless of the subject or the location, I always left feeling that I had been given something. I always felt a little better because of the time spent with her.

And here's something else that in my mind will forever be connected to those conversations — I always left her house either singing or humming the same song:

> There is nothing like a dame
> Nothing in this world.
> There is nothing you can name that is anything
> like a dame.

"Dame" is one of those generational words you don't hear much anymore. I don't think I've ever used it in my life, except as it regarded one woman. Mary Adams was the best dame I've ever known.

When I first met her, we spoke only in passing, usually when I was sitting at her dining table with seven other men who were playing poker when it was Clint's turn to host the game.

It was only after Clint died in 2002 that the lunches and visits with Mary began. I don't remember exactly how they started. I remember only that I was glad they did. I suppose in the beginning, I just wanted to see how she was doing, but it didn't take long before it became clear that I was enjoying the time I spent with her more and more. There were things I could learn from her if I was smart enough to pay attention.

In 2005, I wrote a column about Mary and a long-distance relationship she had going with a man in Texas. It was a marvelous story about love, and it spoke to the irrelevance of age when you found yourself crazy in love. But before I wrote the column, I worried about "trolls" on the Internet, those poor, empty souls who write anonymous attacks for reasons that escape me. I worried that they'd track her email down and fill her Inbox with ugliness.

So I told Mary I wasn't going to identify her or the man in Texas. Here's what she said: "The nice thing about being old is you don't really give a damn what anybody thinks. So do it any way you want. We don't care."

She was the best dame I have ever known. She made something inside of me sing.

The man in Texas was Donald Weisman. He was a college professor, a writer, an artist. After Clinton died in 2002, Mary found a 50-year-old photo snapped on a New York street taken of her and Don. She mailed it to him, and a late-in-life love story bloomed. Jim Belshaw's column about them started out:

She's 84. He's 90. She lives here. He lives in another state. But they know how to get on an airplane and so they have one of those long distance things going, you know?

Don had sent Jim a poem he wrote about his relationship with Mary, which Jim put into this column. Here's the poem Don sent. It's called "Let Me Tell You."

Have you ever
Looked up the meaning
In a big dictionary

of the word home.

You'd be surprised
How richly varied
And subject to ambiguity
That word is,
How it opens up
A virtual vista
Through a little window.

So let me tell you
What I,
A man of ninety,
After lots of loves,
After three wives,
All naturally dead
And mourned,
And children,
Grand children
And great grand children.
All living,
Let me tell you
What has come to mean
Home
To me

It means
Having the rare
Good fortune
Of falling freshly in love,
Deeply,
Body, mind and soul
Right now,
And feeling her easy open invitation
Even as I open to her

And we embrace.

Let me tell you
It's like all the past good
Was a series of markers
Telling me
I was on the right road
Toward that embrace.

And,
Yes,
At last,
All the way
Home.

He's 90. She's 84. They have this long-distance thing going. We should all live so long.

Thanks to Jim Belshaw for sharing his thoughts. Another great love of Mary's life was dance. Her good friend Gigi Bennahum will now share some stories.

Gigi Bennahum speaks.

Mary was so proud of her granddaughter Devon, a dancer since she was a little girl. Today we are honored to have Devon perform her dance, "Oh My Soul," in honor of her grandmother. The psalm readers are her siblings, Ian, Gray and Kayla.

Dance, music, readings

A Meditation on Psalm 90

Lord, what are we, that You have regard for us? What are we, that You are mindful of us? A thousand years in your sight are like a day that has just gone by, or like a watch in the night.

We are like a breath; our days are as a passing shadow; we come and go like grass which in the morning shoots up, renewed, and in the evening fades and withers.

You cause us to revert to dust, saying: Return, o mortal creatures! Would that we were wise, that we understood whither we are going! For when we die, we carry nothing away; our glory does not accompany us.

Our days may come to 70 years, or 80 if our strength endures. They quickly pass and we fly away. Teach us to number our days, that we may gain a heart of wisdom.

Mark the whole-hearted and behold the upright; they shall have peace. Lord, You redeem the soul of Your servants, and none who trust in You shall be desolate.

May the favor of the Lord our God rest on us; establish the work of our hands for us — yes, establish the work of our hands.

Mary Adams' strength endured for 91 years. She was as sharp as ever right up to the end. The work of her hands and mind and heart will endure in ways beyond our knowing. We affirm that her love endures in the lives she touched.

Parents give us roots and give us wings. They bring us into the world, provide a foundation and then give us the tools to find our own way. Though we may have grown up and grown away, there is still something special about sharing our victories and commiserating our defeats with that special parent figure in our lives. Even if the relationship might have been challenging at different moments, we never stray far from the promise that home is where the heart is.

Losing a parent, even after a long and full life, leaves an empty place in our hearts. In spite of the darkness cast by this loss, we reaffirm our belief in the light of life.

If you would like to join in the reading of the 23rd Psalm, the text is on the inside of your program.

Recitation of the 23rd Psalm

Closing Thoughts

The time is now 5:12 p.m. At Mary's house, that would mean it was cocktail time. Her favorite drink was a vodka martini with as many olives as she could get away with. Second place was Irish whiskey.

There's an Irish ditty that goes:

> There are many good reasons for drinking. One has just entered my head.
> If a man doesn't drink when he's living, how the hell can he drink when he's dead?

I have a special memorial gift for you to take home with you. This cocktail napkin has Mary's name, date of birth, date of death, and a martini glass with two olives. Please take one or two as you leave, and raise a toast to Mary as you enjoy your favorite beverage over the next few days.

Let us finish our service with an Irish blessing:

> These things, I warmly wish for you —
> Someone to love, some work to do,
> A bit of o' sun, a bit o' cheer.
> And a guardian angel always near.

Mary Adams is now our guardian angel. Keep her memory burning bright in your heart. And keep telling her stories. As long as we remember the lives of those we love, they never truly die. As David Marshall plays "Amazing Grace," please allow the family to exit first. They look forward to greeting you outside the chapel.

Bagpiper – "Amazing Grace"

You can see a video of this service on YouTube at:
http://youtu.be/QxKekXHKIV4.

MEMORIAL SERVICE FOR LINDA LEE FOX

This memorial service took place in the yard and garden of the home of the woman who died. Rows of rented folding chairs filled the lawn, a screen and projector was set up inside a large tent that also served as the buffet area, and a balloon launch was held after the viewing of the tribute video.

Introduction

Before we start today's celebration of the life of Linda Lee Fox, please help us maintain the sacredness of this time by silencing or turning off your electronic devices. Please rise as you are able to welcome Linda's family.

Family brings flowers to the vase next to Linda's picture.

Welcome. I am Certified Celebrant Gail Rubin. Thank you for coming today to help honor and celebrate the beautiful life of a special woman, Linda Lee Fox. Your presence is a welcome gift in support of her family.

Linda loved to nurture her plants and yard, including this gorgeous willow tree we gather under today. Linda planted this willow tree with her family when they first moved to this home in 1988.

She also loved to nurture her family with love and care — husband Richard; sons Dennis and John; daughters-in-law Donna, Jordan and Shawn; daughters-in-love Misty and Shayna; and her grandchildren, Kyle, Chloe, Addie, Hillary, Nicholas and Cameron.

Unfortunately, a brain tumor first bedeviled Linda five years ago. It happened during one of her many trips to Puerto Vallarta, Mexico, with Richard. It was a place they always greatly enjoyed visiting. Surgery and other treatments helped reduce the size of the tumor, but it eventually grew back. Over the past few months, as the tumor took its toll on her, Linda was lovingly supported by her family here at the home she so loved.

Linda was: Strong. Independent. Vibrant. Supportive. Helpful. Giving. And so much more.

Linda was born in Des Moines, Iowa, on January 28, 1949, as Linda Lee Yarman. She moved to California with her new adopted family that included brother Michael and sister Patty.

It was in California years later that she met her first husband John Patrick Sheffer — you would know him as Pat. They met at a USO dance when she was 17 and he was 18. Pat was just getting ready to ship out to Vietnam. She waited 18 months for him to return from his tour of duty.

Linda and Pat got married in 1969 and moved to Pat's hometown of Alamogordo. It was there they had their first son, Dennis William Sheffer, in 1969. When Dennis was 5, the family moved to Albuquerque, where son John Michael

Sheffer was born in 1982. Linda and Pat divorced years later.

Linda always loved dancing, and dancing once again brought a husband into her life. Linda met Richard Fox, the love of her life, at the Caravan East nightclub. They married 17 years ago in 1996 and built a beautiful life and business together.

She was a legal secretary in Albuquerque. After meeting Richard, they both made a shift toward real estate entrepreneurship, buying and rehabbing properties to rent out.

Linda was meticulous with the houses, as she was in all facets of her life. At first, Linda and Richard did all the work themselves. Eventually, they found talented people to help. This did not, however, stop Linda from always checking the work and making sure it was perfect. From the flowers on the front door to the windows being cleaned just right, her careful eye caught all the details.

Good health and self-improvement were important to Linda. Healthy eating and exercise were a big part of her life. She took up body building in the late 1990s. You can see a picture of Linda in her prime in the reception area. She is a model we can all strive to emulate.

If you had a health question, she knew just the right supplement to take. She would not only tell you about the supplement; she would go get it for you. She was the first to know all about the newest workouts and diets.

Mentally and physically, she had a commitment to excellence. She and Richard would go on retreats to improve their human potential. She walked on broken glass, broke an arrow with her throat, and ate fire. You can see the photos of her achieving these feats in the tribute video we'll show later.

Linda and Richard loved to travel, including their many trips to Mexico, to China, and to see Richard's family in New Orleans. But it was always great to come back home to Albuquerque, to have a glass of wine by the fire and enjoy her home and yard.

She loved her animals very much, and she had as many as three dogs and 10 cats at one point. She rescued neighborhood stray cats and got them spayed and neutered. She even had Richard build them their own special cat condo in the garage.

She loved people as much as she loved animals. Linda was accepting of everyone. At Thanksgiving and Christmas, if you didn't have somewhere to go, her door was always open for you.

Linda loved this yard that we gather in today. She loved playing with her kids and grandchildren in it. She loved watching her dog Shadow run around with his toys. She loved tending to her flowers and plants. Her favorite flowers were irises and roses. And look, they bloom for her today.

She would always bring a touch of beauty to her surroundings: flowers on the door, a candle on the table, a colored glass bottle on a window ledge or other unique yin-yangs, as she called them. Thrift-store shopping was a thrill for Linda. She loved taking her family and friends to all the different dollar stores and Savers.

She was very graceful and giving. Even after she got sick, she made sure you were taken care of. She was always sending you home with a care package with just about anything you needed — socks, underwear, food, money and more. She would always find a way to help you.

We will now hear from Linda's family members. After they

speak, if you have a story about Linda you would like to share, you will have a chance to come forward and speak.

Comments by:
1. *Richard Fox*
2. *Dennis Sheffer*
3. *John Sheffer*
4. *Donna Sheffer*
5. *Misty Oracion*
6. *Shayna Ernest*

Open comments

Linda Lee Fox danced through this life with good energy. And as we know from physics, energy does not disappear; it merely changes form. Although Linda's physical presence has gone from our sight, her loving energy continues on in our hearts and minds, and will continue to live on as long as we live and remember her.

Let us resolve to go forth from today's service inspired to live better lives thanks to Linda's example. To dance for the joy of movement and expression of energy ... to care for all creatures great and small, people, plants and animals ... to nurture growth and to find the best in ourselves and others.

The family has prepared this video photomontage of Linda's life.

Show video photomontage.

Balloon Release

To help release Linda's spirit and raise our own, we will now do a balloon release in her honor. Know that these are biodegradable balloons, so the environment will not be harmed by this balloon launch. We will then have a reception where we can continue the conversation, dance, and eat carrot cake, which was Linda's favorite.

Please allow the family to gather their balloons first. Once each person here has a balloon, we will do a countdown and release them all at once, with love and joy, in Linda's honor. Again, thank you for your presence here today.

Following the Service

After the balloon launch, the attendees enjoyed a buffet luncheon and sat at tables under the willow tree Linda Lee Fox had planted and nurtured. Recorded music played through the speaker system set up for the event.

Some of her cremated remains were later scattered throughout the garden around the house. Many months later, her husband, Richard, took the remainder to Puerto Vallarta, Mexico. A group of family and friends scattered the rest of her remains there in the ocean during the Dia de los Muertos (Day of the Dead) celebration.

You can see a video of this service on YouTube at:
http://youtu.be/mO6xiWnpDEY.

6

READINGS, MUSIC AND RESOURCES

MEMORIAL READINGS AND POEMS

Do Not Stand at My Grave and Weep

Do not stand at my grave and weep,
I am not there, I do not sleep.
I am a thousand winds that blow,
I am the diamond glints on snow.
I am the sunlight on ripened grain,
I am the gentle autumn rain.
When you awaken in the morning's hush
I am the swift uplifting rush
Of quiet birds in circling flight.
I am the soft star-shine at night.
Do not stand at my grave and cry;
I am not there; I did not die.

—*Mary Elizabeth Frye*

Funeral Blues

Stop all the clocks, cut off the telephone,
Prevent the dog from barking with a juicy bone,
Silence the pianos and with muffled drum
Bring out the coffin, let the mourners come.

Let aeroplanes circle moaning overhead
Scribbling on the sky the message He Is Dead,
Put crêpe bows round the white necks of the public doves,
Let the traffic policemen wear black cotton gloves.

He was my North, my South, my East and West,
My working week and my Sunday-rest,
My noon, my midnight, my talk, my song;
I thought that love would last for ever: I was wrong.

The stars are not wanted now: put out every one;
Pack up the moon and dismantle the sun;
Pour away the ocean and sweep up the wood.
For nothing now can ever come to any good.

—*W.H. Auden*

Thanatopsis – Final Verse

So live that when thy summons comes to join
The innumerable caravan, which moves
To that mysterious realm, where each shall take
His chamber in the silent halls of death,
Thou go not, like the quarry-slave at night,
Scourged to his dungeon, but, sustained and soothed
By an unfaltering trust, approach thy grave
Like one who wraps the drapery of his couch
About him, and lies down to pleasant dreams.

—*William Cullen Bryant*

Because I Could Not Stop for Death

Because I could not stop for Death —
He kindly stopped for me —
The Carriage held but just Ourselves —
And Immortality.

We slowly drove — He knew no haste
And I had put away
My labor and my leisure too,
For his civility —

We passed the School, where Children strove
At Recess — in the Ring —
We passed the Fields of Gazing Grain —
We passed the Setting Sun —

Or rather — He passed Us —
The Dews drew quivering and Chill —
For only Gossamer, my Gown —
My Tippet — only Tulle —

We paused before a House that seemed —
A Swelling of the Ground —
The Roof was scarcely visible —
The Cornice — in the Ground —

Since then — 'tis Centuries — and yet
Feels shorter than the Day
I first surmised the Horses' Heads
Were toward eternity —

—Emily Dickinson

The Peace Prayer of St. Francis of Assisi

Lord, make me an instrument of your peace;
Where there is hatred, let me sow love;
Where there is injury, pardon;
Where there is doubt, faith;
Where there is despair, hope;
Where there is darkness, light;
And where there is sadness, joy.

O Divine Master,
Grant that I may not so much seek
To be consoled as to console;
To be understood as to understand;
To be loved as to love.

For it is in giving that we receive;
it is in pardoning that we are pardoned;
and it is in dying that we are born to eternal life.

Death as the Birthday of Your Eternity

Look forward without fear to that appointed hour — the last hour of
the body but not of the soul. That day, which you fear as the end of
all things, is the birthday of your eternity.

—Seneca

All the World's a Stage

All the world's a stage,
And all the men and women merely players;
They have their exits and their entrances;
And one man in his time plays many parts,
His acts being seven ages. At first, the infant,

Mewling and puking in the nurse's arms;
Then the whining school-boy, with his satchel
And shining morning face, creeping like snail
Unwillingly to school. And then the lover,
Sighing like furnace, with a woeful ballad
Made to his mistress' eyebrow. Then a soldier,
Full of strange oaths and bearded like the pard,
Jealous in honour, sudden and quick in quarrel,
Seeking the bubble reputation
Even in the cannon's mouth. And then the justice,
In fair round belly with good capon lin'd,
With eyes severe and beard of formal cut,
Full of wise saws and modern instances;
And so he plays his part. The sixth age shifts
Into the lean and slipper'd pantaloon,
With spectacles on nose and pouch on side,
His youthful hose, well sav'd, a world too wide
For his shrunk shank; and his big manly voice,
Turning again toward childish treble, pipes
And whistles in his sound. Last scene of all,
That ends this strange eventful history,
Is second childishness and mere oblivion;
Sans teeth, sans eyes, sans taste, sans every thing.

—*William Shakespeare, "As You Like It," Act II, Scene VII*

Death

Then Almitra spoke, saying, "We would ask now of Death." And he said:

You would know the secret of death. But how shall you find it unless you seek it in the heart of life? The owl whose night-bound eyes are blind unto the day cannot unveil the mystery of light. If you would indeed behold the spirit of death, open your heart wide unto the body

97

of life. For life and death are one, even as the river and the sea are one. In the depth of your hopes and desires lies your silent knowledge of the beyond; And like seeds dreaming beneath the snow your heart dreams of spring. Trust the dreams, for in them is hidden the gate to eternity.

Your fear of death is but the trembling of the shepherd when he stands before the king whose hand is to be laid upon him in honour. Is the shepherd not joyful beneath his trembling, that he shall wear the mark of the king? Yet is he not more mindful of his trembling?

For what is it to die but to stand naked in the wind and to melt into the sun? And what is it to cease breathing, but to free the breath from its restless tides, that it may rise and expand and seek God unencumbered?

Only when you drink from the river of silence shall you indeed sing. And when you have reached the mountain top, then you shall begin to climb. And when the earth shall claim your limbs, then shall you truly dance.

—*Kahlil Gibran, "The Prophet"*

READINGS FOR OUTDOOR/SEASIDE CEREMONIES

Thanatopsis (opening excerpt)

To him who in the love of Nature holds
Communion with her visible forms, she speaks
A various language; for his gayer hours
She has a voice of gladness, and a smile
And eloquence of beauty, and she glides
Into his darker musings, with a mild
And healing sympathy, that steals away
Their sharpness, ere he is aware. When thoughts

Of the last bitter hour come like a blight
Over thy spirit, and sad images
Of the stern agony, and shroud, and pall,
And breathless darkness, and the narrow house,
Make thee shudder, and grow sick at heart; —
Go forth under the open sky, and list
To Nature's teachings, while from all around —
Earth and her waters, and the depths of air —
Comes a still voice —

—*William Cullen Bryant*

What Is Dying?

I am standing upon the seashore. A ship at my side spreads her white sails to the morning breeze, and starts for the blue ocean. She is an object of beauty and strength, and I stand and watch until at last she hangs like a speck of white cloud just where the sea and sky come down to meet and mingle with each other. Then someone at my side says, "There! She's gone!" Gone where? Gone from my sight — that is all. She is just as large in mast and hull and spar as she was when she left my side, and just as able to bear her load of living freight to the place of her destination. Her diminished size is in me, not in her.

And just at the moment when someone at my side says, "There! She's gone!" there are other eyes watching her coming; and other voices ready to take up the glad shout: "There she comes!"

And that is — "dying."

—*This reading has been attributed to both*
  Henry Van Dyke, as A Parable of Immortality,
  and as What Is Dying? by Luther F. Beecher

Crossing the Bar

Sunset and evening star,
    And one clear call for me!
And may there be no moaning of the bar,
    When I put out to sea.

But such a tide as moving seems asleep,
    Too full for sound or foam,
When that which drew from out the boundless deep
    Turns again home.

Twilight and evening bell,
    And after that the dark!
And may there be no sadness of farewell,
    When I embark;

For tho' from out our bourne of Time and Place
    The flood may bear me far,
I hope to see my Pilot face to face,
    When I have crost the bar.

    —*Alfred, Lord Tennyson*

Sonnet XVIII

Shall I compare thee to a summer's day?
Thou art more lovely and more temperate:
Rough winds do shake the darling buds of May,
And summer's lease hath all too short a date:
Sometime too hot the eye of heaven shines,
And often is his gold complexion dimm'd;
And every fair from fair sometime declines,
By chance or nature's changing course untrimm'd:
But thy eternal summer shall not fade,

Nor lose possession of that fair thou ow'st;
Nor shall Death brag thou wander'st in his shade,
When in eternal lines to time thou grow'st,
So long as men can breathe or eyes can see,
So long lives this, and this gives life to thee.

—*William Shakespeare*

Death Is Not Extinguishing the Light

Death is not extinguishing the light;
It is only putting out the lamp because the dawn has come.

—*Sir Rabindranath Tagore*

MUSIC FOR SERVICES

There are so many songs that can make a meaningful contribution to a memorial service. You don't need to stick to religious chestnuts such as "Amazing Grace" and "How Great Thou Art." Consider these out-of-the-ordinary musical suggestions to enhance the laughter and tears.

Quirky Songs

If the deceased was known for having a sense of humor, one of these songs might be just right for the memorial service:

- "Always Look on the Bright Side of Life," by Eric Idle (from "Life of Brian" and "Spamalot")
- "And When I Die," by Laura Nyro, performed by Three Dog Night and others
- "Another One Bites the Dust," by John Deacon, performed by Queen
- "Bat Out of Hell," by Jim Steinman, performed by Meat Loaf
- "Highway to Hell," by Bon Scott, Angus Young and Malcolm Young, performed by AC/DC
- "I'm Going Home," by Richard O'Brien, performed by Tim Curry (from "The Rocky Horror Picture Show")

- "Just a Gigolo"/"I Ain't Got Nobody" medley, performed by David Lee Roth ("Just a Gigolo" lyrics by Julius Brammer and music by Leonello Casucci; "I Ain't Got Nobody" lyrics by Roger A. Graham and music by Spencer Williams)
- "Leader of the Pack," by George Morton, Jeff Barry and Ellie Greenwich, performed by The Shangri-Las
- "My Way," by Paul Anka, performed by Frank Sinatra and others
- "Please Don't Bury Me," by John Prine
- "(Don't Fear) The Reaper," by Donald Roeser, performed by Blue Öyster Cult
- "Spirit in the Sky," by Norman Greenbaum
- "That's Life," by Dean Kay and Kelly Gordon, performed by Frank Sinatra

Pop Songs

The definition of a pop song varies, depending on when one comes of age. These songs were popular in different eras, but they all have a sentimental theme that may bring a tear to the eye.

- "100 Years," by John Ondrasik, performing as Five for Fighting
- "Climb Ev'ry Mountain," music by Richard Rodgers and lyrics by Oscar Hammerstein II, performed by various artists (from "The Sound of Music")
- "Both Sides Now," by Joni Mitchell
- "Bridge Over Troubled Water," by Paul Simon, performed by Simon and Garfunkel
- "Forever Young," by Bob Dylan
- "Forever Young," by Rod Stewart, Jim Cregan, Kevin Savigar and Bob Dylan, recorded by various artists
- "Have I Told You Lately," by Van Morrison, recorded by various artists
- "If I Die Young," by Kimberly Perry, recorded by The Band Perry
- "In My Life," by John Lennon and Paul McCartney, performed by The Beatles

- "Living Years," by Mike Rutherford and B.A. Robertson, performed by Mike + The Mechanics
- "Over The Rainbow," music by Harold Arlen and lyrics by E.Y. Harburg, performed by various artists (from "The Wizard of Oz")
- "The Rose," by Amanda McBroom, performed by Bette Midler
- "Smoke Gets in Your Eyes," music by Jerome Kern and lyrics by Otto Harbach, performed by various artists
- "Stormy Weather," music by Harold Arlen and lyrics by Ted Koehler, performed by various artists
- "Tears in Heaven," by Eric Clapton and Will Jennings
- "We'll Meet Again," by Ross Parker and Hughie Charles, performed by various artists
- "Wind Beneath My Wings," by Jeff Silbar and Larry Henley, performed by Bette Midler
- "Yesterday," by John Lennon and Paul McCartney, performed by The Beatles
- "You've Got a Friend," by Carole King

Traditional Songs and Ballads

You can find a number of different recordings of these traditional songs, hymns and ballads related to funerals, death, partings, loss and hope. Many of these songs are so old that their origins are obscure, and all have been recorded by a variety of different performers.

- "Amazing Grace," lyrics by John Newton
- "Finnegan's Wake"
- "El Paso," by Marty Robbins (featured in the "Breaking Bad" finale episode, "Felina")
- "I'll Fly Away," by Albert E. Brumley
- "Red River Valley"
- "St. James Infirmary Blues"
- "Streets of Laredo"
- "Swing Low, Sweet Chariot," by Wallace Willis
- "The Water is Wide"

- "The Wayfaring Stranger"
- "This Train"
- "When the Saints Go Marching In," music by Virgil O. Stamps and lyrics by Luther G. Presley
- "Will the Circle Be Unbroken," music by Charles H. Gabriel and lyrics by Ada R. Habersohn
- "You Are My Sunshine," by Jimmie Davis and Charles Mitchell

ONLINE RESOURCES

The following websites offer a variety of resources that may be helpful in planning a memorial service.

Poems and Readings

If you're looking for an inspirational quote, poem or reading, try one of these sites:

- All Poetry: allpoetry.com
- BrainyQuote: www.brainyquote.com
- Favorite Poets and Poems: www.famouspoetsandpoems.com
- Great-Quotes.com: www.great-quotes.com
- Linda's Lyrics, LLC: www.thedashpoem.com
- PoemHunter.com: www.poemhunter.com
- Poetry Soup: www.poetrysoup.com
- The Quotations Page: www.quotationspage.com
- The Quote Garden: quotegarden.com

Music Downloads

Here are a few sites for downloading music that you might want to use in a memorial service. Some of the music is available for free and some requires a fee.

- Amazon: www.amazon.com
- EMD Music: easymusicdownload.com
- iTunes: www.apple.com/itunes

- Music Downloads: www.musicdownloads.com
- Softonic: download-free-music.en.softonic.com

Information and Services

The following organizations offer a wealth of useful information related to funeral, memorial and end-of-life planning:

- A Good Goodbye: Funeral Planning for Those Who Don't Plan to Die: www.AGoodGoodbye.com
- American Academy of Estate Planning Attorneys: www.AAEPA.com
- American Association of Tissue Banks: www.AATB.org
- Association for Death Education and Counseling: www.ADEC.org
- Be Remembered (free site for memorialization): www.BeRemembered.com
- Celebrant Foundation & Institute (Personalized life cycle celebrant training and directory): www.celebrantinstitute.org
- Compassion & Choices (end-of-life education, counseling and advocacy): www.CompassionandChoices.org
- Cremation Association of North America: www.CremationAssociation.org
- Death Cafe (discuss death over tea and cake): www.DeathCafe.com
- Death Over Dinner (discuss death at a dinner party): www.DeathOverDinner.org
- Everest Funeral Planning and Concierge Service (PriceFinderSM funeral home price comparison report): www.EverestFuneral.com
- Five Wishes (a booklet for expressing advance medical directives): www.AgingWithDignity.org
- Funeral Consumers Alliance (an organization dedicated to ensuring that consumers can choose a meaningful, dignified and affordable funeral): www.Funerals.org
- Funeralwise.com ("Everything you need to know about funerals"): www.Funeralwise.com

- Green Burial Council (information on environmentally sustainable death care): www.GreenBurialCouncil.org
- Have The Talk of a Lifetime (how to remember and honor loved ones): www.HaveTheTalkofaLifetime.org
- I'm Sorry To Hear (online funeral planning tools and advice): www.ImSorryToHear.com
- In The Light Urns: www.InTheLightUrns.com
- International Cemetery, Cremation and Funeral Association: www.ICCFA.com
- In-Sight Institute (national resource for Certified Funeral Celebrants): www.InSightBooks.com
- Katzman Monument Company: www.KatzmanMonument.com
- Life Legacy (whole body donation program): www.LifeLegacy.org
- Meaningful Funerals (why funerals and memorial services are important): www.MeaningfulFunerals.com
- MedCure (whole body donation program): www.MedCure.org
- National Funeral Directors Association: www.NFDA.org
- National Home Funeral Alliance: www.HomeFuneralAlliance.org
- Science Care (whole body donation program): www.ScienceCare.com
- Selected Independent Funeral Homes: www.SelectedFuneralHomes.org
- Shopping for Funeral Services, Federal Trade Commission: www.consumer.ftc.gov/articles/0070-shopping-funeral-services
- The Conversation Project: www.TheConversationProject.org

Acknowledgements

Acknowledgements from Gail Rubin

Thanks to Michael Adams, Richard Fox and Richard Warren and their families for allowing me to share the scripts of the memorial services for their loved ones. It was an honor to work with you and celebrate each person's remarkable life.

Big hugs and kisses to my husband, David Bleicher, for his support and encouragement. Death lives at our house, and we're good with that.

And to those who have crossed over to The Great Beyond, thank you for the love and wisdom you shared in this lifetime. You are remembered and live on in my heart.

Acknowledgments from Susan Fraser

Thank you to Larry Moss, Bob Cibulskis, and Earl McKee Jr., and their families for allowing us to share the stories of their loved ones memorial services. It is an honor to be able to share these stories with other grieving families who can relate.

Much appreciation and love to my son, Tyler Fraser, we couldn't be more proud or thankful for all you do in your own business as well as ours.

A big pat on the back to our content director Erica Cassano who worked very hard with us to make this book a reality.

Last but not least, a big thank you to the families that our staff has the pleasure to meet and serve each day, it is an honor to work with each and every one of you.

ABOUT THE AUTHORS

GAIL RUBIN

Gail Rubin, CT, The Doyenne of Death,® helps get end-of-life and funeral planning conversations started with a light touch on serious subjects. She's the author and host of the award-winning book and TV/DVD series, *A Good Goodbye: Funeral Planning for Those Who Don't Plan to Die.*

An engaging, award-winning speaker, she uses humor and funny films to attract people to a topic many would rather avoid. She "knocked 'em dead" at TEDxABQ in September 2015 with a laugh-filled talk about undertaking pre-need end-of-life planning.

Gail pioneered the Death Cafe movement in the United States by hosting the first one west of the Mississippi in September 2012. Her motto is, "Talking about sex won't make you pregnant, talking about funerals won't make you dead."

Rubin is a Certified Thanatologist, a designation awarded by the Association for Death Education and Counseling and a fancy name for a death educator. She is also a Certified Celebrant, a Life Tribute professional personally trained by Doug Manning and Glenda Stansbury of the In-Sight Institute, the leading U.S. organization that trains funeral Celebrants.

She is a member of the Association for Death Education and Counseling, the International Cemetery, Cremation and Funeral Association, the National Speakers Association New Mexico Chapter and Toastmasters International.

She volunteers with the *Chevra Kaddisha*, a group that ritually prepares the bodies of Jews for burial, and she serves on the cemetery committee for her synagogue, Congregation Albert in Albuquerque, NM. She is also a leader of the New Mexico Interfaith Dialogue.

Gail has been interviewed about funeral planning issues in national and local broadcast, print and online media. Outlets include *The Huffington Post*, *Money Magazine*, *Kiplinger*, CBS Radio News, WGN-TV, and local affiliates for NPR, PBS, FOX, ABC-TV, CBS-TV and NBC-TV.

Download a free planning form and the free eBook *Celebrating Life: How to Create Meaningful Memorial Services, with Templates and Tips* at her website, www.AGoodGoodbye.com.

SUSAN FRASER

Susan Fraser, a respected authority of the funeral industry, has dedicated the last couple decades to ensuring that when a loved one is lost, their memory is not. She is the founder of United Priority Distributors, a wholesale cremation urn company, as well as founder and CEO of In the Light Urns, In the Light Caskets, and Pets to Rest ecommerce memorial product companies.

In the summer of 1995, Fraser and her husband were faced with a heavy loss. Their eldest son, Ryan, passed away very unexpectedly from an undiagnosed heart condition. This of course was an extremely difficult time for them and their other son, Tyler. For the six years that followed, Fraser found her passion for helping others who suffered the loss of a loved one, whether it be sudden or expected.

In 2001, Fraser was one of the first persons to begin an online company that offers the distribution and manufacturing of memorial urns, keepsakes and cremation jewelry. Her company, In the Light Urns, has been recognized for their outstanding products by a number of popular media outlets such as CNBC news channel, National Funeral Directors Association (NFDA) TV, USA Today news channel, The Today Show on NBC, and TIME Magazine.

Fraser is a member of the International Cemetery, Cremation and Funeral Association, along with the National Funeral Directors Association. She is a partner of 501C3 non-profit organizations such as Jalen's Gift Foundation, a company that assists grieving loved ones after the loss of an infant, child, newborn, stillborn or miscarriage, and Strong as Jamie; supporting those facing the tough battle of cancer. Fraser's is also the first and only online company to offer free cremation urns to those who absolutely can't afford one, through her company In the Light Urns.

Find out more about the products and what she has to offer at any of her websites, www.InTheLightUrns.com, www.PetsToRest.com, and www.InTheLightCaskets.com.

PRODUCTS FROM
A GOOD GOODBYE AND LIGHT TREE PRESS

A Good Goodbye:
Funeral Planning for Those Who Don't Plan to Die

This award-winning book provides the information, inspiration and tools to plan and implement creative, meaningful and memorable end-of-life rituals for people and their pets. **A Good Goodbye** addresses the Baby Boomer generation with gentle humor on the vital information about funeral arrangements that most people don't learn about until faced with a death in the family. $21.95 print/$9.99 eBook

The award-winning TV interview series on a 4-DVD set presents an educational and entertaining 12-episode series of 30-minute programs with expert interviews on "everything you need to know before you go." From pre-need planning to grief counseling, financial issues to the latest trends in death care, including pet loss, celebrant services and green funerals, these interviews offer eye-opening insights into the party no one wants to plan. $49.97

The Newly-Dead Game®

The Newly-Dead Game® helps start funeral planning conversations in a fun, non-threatening way. The game is based on elements of the classic TV game show *The Newlywed Game*, but the questions in The Newly-Dead Game® revolve around how well the couple knows each other's last wishes. $24.97

The Family Plot File

When time is of the essence, can you easily assemble the names, addresses, emails and phone numbers for all your family and friends?

PRODUCTS FROM
A GOOD GOODBYE AND LIGHT TREE PRESS

The Family Plot File electronic data resource will help you organize contacts for your family and friends and make holding life cycle events so much easier! $29.99

"Time Flies" blank note cards

"Time Flies" note cards are perfect for saying "Thank you," "My condolences," "Happy birthday," and "Thought you might find this of interest." This artistic card features an image of an hourglass with wings set inside an ornate circle. The image came from a photo taken of a crypt gate in the historic Woodland Cemetery in Stamford, CT, established in 1859. Comes in packages of 12 with envelopes. $15.00

Stainless steel pendants for cremated remains

People can keep the cremated remains of their loved ones, whether people or pets, close to the heart with these stylish stainless steel chamber pendants. Each sleek and sturdy stainless steel pendant works well as jewelry for both men and women, with a dozen designs from which to choose. These affordable keepsake pendants allow large families to share their loved ones' remains among many relatives. $18.95 per pendant
$7.95 additional for an 18" stainless steel box chain

Visit the Online Store at www.AGoodGoodbye.com to order today!

Gail Rubin is available as a Funeral Celebrant in Albuquerque, New Mexico. She also consults with families who want an informed advocate for pre-need funeral planning and she is a licensed agent selling insurance for final expenses and home health care coverage.

CPSIA information can be obtained
at www.ICGtesting.com
Printed in the USA
FSOW04n2159241215
14580FS